To Diego
with love
Pilar

28/03/2023

The **PILGRIM BRIDE**

Is a second marriage better than the first?

Pilar Cerón Durán

The Muse of the Atacama Desert, Chile.

Cover and back cover design: Gisela BC Design

English interpreter: Ariadna Carobene. Workana

Spanish corrections: Maite Ayala https://www.facebook.com/maite.ayala.77

English trailer: Lucas Rosatto, Video editing lrosatto1@gmail.com

Song "So in Love": music, lyrics and interpretation, William M. Elías. RN: PAu003842409

ISBN: 9798511978642

The novel ***The Pilgrim Bride. Is a first marriage better than the second?*** is a smart book.

What is a smart book?

A smart book is considered to be one that contains certain QR codes and links inside, through which it is possible to interact with the author and access extra information that enriches the reading, either through videos, pictures, voice notes, messages written by the author, and it's even possible to communicate through WhatsApp.

To access, you must capture with your camera, which can be from your cell phone, the QR code that appears on each page, press the read option that will show up and, that will you give access to the connected link.

Readers who wish to access more information and delve into the transcendental chapters, more impacting and fun scenes and learn about the behind the scenes of the literary work, will have the privilege to share with the author, with some of the other characters and other readers, in a monthly Zoom meeting that will take place on the last Wednesday day of each month, from 7:00 p.m. to 8:00 p.m., London, England time, being able to participate those who purchase the novel that month to participate and send a personal photo with the book, via email or WhatsApp.

I hope you enjoy it and that this may be the beginning of a formidable friendship between you, my favourite reader, and I, the writer, your long distance friend.

DEDICATION

The Pilgrim Bride. Is a second marriage better than the first? is a novel dedicated to all, men and women, who find themselves trapped in a suffocating relationship. It's a story about strength, overcoming and happiness, despite adversities. It conveys hope and confidence in life, in the spirit that's always there to pick the body up and say to the soul: "you can do it". And in love that, although elusive, can also be found just around the corner, because it's about learning to live, going with the flow and leaving everything behind in search of happiness, sometimes so avoidable and yet so worth it.

I trust that Esmeralda's experiences will light your journey in the search for freedom, allowing you a new rebirth of happiness and love.

ACKNOWLEDGMENTS

My deepest gratitude goes to the wonderful people that I've had the privilege and honour of getting to know and enjoying their friendship, their company and unconditional support, in my joys and sadness, in my failures and success, in moments of turmoil and calm, being the source of my inspiration and indispensable strength to regain my freedom and happiness: without all of you, the life of the pilgrim bride would never have been written.

All my love and gratitude goes out to each and every one of you, and especially to my mother.

ABOUT THE AUTHOR

Pilar Cerón Durán

The Muse of the Atacama Desert, Chile.

Born in Pichidegua, Region of the Liberator General Bernardo O'Higgins Riquelme, Chile, in 1963, being an adoptive daughter of Copiapó, Region of Atacama. She completed her university studies obtaining her Bachelor's degree in Social Work and a Master's in Business Administration, MBA. She grew up in the countryside, which fostered a special connection with nature and animals. Since a young age, she's had an adroitness to write, reflecting a powerful imagination. ***The Pilgrim Bride. Is a second marriage better than the first?*** is the first novel and literary work that she has published.

LINKS TO CONTACT THE AUTHOR

Email: pilarceronduran@gmail.com

Facebook fan page: https://acortar.link/ZAax1

Instagram: https://www.instagram.com/

YouTube channel: https://n9.cl/q8iw1

WhatsApp: https://wa.me/qr/CIUJYBAU73CWK1

Trailer The Pilgrim Bride

The **PILGRIM BRIDE**

Is a second marriage better than the first?

Pilar Cerón Durán

The Muse of the Atacama Desert, Chile.

INTRODUCTION

The Pilgrim Bride

Is a second marriage better than the first?

The main character of the love story ***The Pilgrim Bride. Is a second marriage better than the first?*** is a fifty-something-year-old divorcee, beautiful as the sunrise, with a defiant, energetic, radiant, passionate and voracious personality. A cyclone, and enemy of routines, she is a lover of freedom, of love itself and of her family, who despite her successful professional career, makes a drastic change in her personal life when she decides to study English in London. She leaves everything behind, from the memories of her unfortunate marriage until the blessed divorce, including her family, friends, loved ones and her beloved Atacama homeland covered in multi-coloured hills, pristine dunes and extraordinary beaches with golden sand and crystal waters. This decision will take her on a journey to the Old World, to venture and enjoy spellbinding experiences in the Anglo-Saxon lands, with thousands of adventures, to rediscover love, which wasn't in her plans, and even less to become a bride once again, get married and wear white like a virgin, an unusual event if you take into account that at her first wedding she wore strictly black. If there's a before and after in our protagonist's life, the 180-degree turn in her life will shock you and bring you to tears: from a submissive woman, living under the oppression of a miner husband – abusive and misogynist, managing to escape and freeing herself from a hell she was submerged in, being reborn into a new life with her own light, without prejudice or bonds to erroneous family customs and traditions – like "you only marry once and it's for forever", "You cannot wear red, that colour isn't for a decent woman such as yourself", and don't even think about divorce, a truly forbidden topic, recalcitrant nonsense. These castrators of freedom, love and happiness, being false beliefs of which she happily lets go, red becoming one of her favourite colours, catapulting her worldwide not only as the Pilgrim Bride, but also envied for her "Magical red shoes".

In her new life, the Pilgrim Bride once again smiles, is happy and spontaneous; after regaining her self-esteem, her freedom and independence, she begins to shine and blossom, to enjoy happiness and love in a holistic sense, and nature, as well as developing a taste for exquisite delicacies such as Scotch whisky, and oysters with lemon – in the company of a few intellectual and visionary friends. A precedent and trendsetter, for whom there are no limits, no no's nor paths with dead ends.

This story will shock you and bring you laughter; her experiences as a woman, lover, wife, mother and grandmother will make you cry and move you; you will hurt due to the injustices and outrageous events she will endure and overcome on her journey through Santiago de Chile and Rio de Janeiro after being deported from Heathrow Airport in London; you will feel the hurt of the impossibility of being able to live and share with her children, and being prohibited from seeing and enjoying the love of her grandchildren; you will be happy and surprised by the annulment of her church marriage granted by the church hierarchy; and lastly, you will be moved to tears as you see the long-awaited-for reunion with her love and her stupendous ending.

The book will provoke an irresistible desire to flip back the pages and relive the Pilgrim Bride's adventures, fallings-out and ups-and-downs, over and over again.

TABLE OF CONTENTS

CHAPTER I

A drastic breaking point in her personal life

It was a warm morning in late July, something wonderful and unusual in mid-winter. The sun shone high above the mountaintops, heightening the arid and colourful Atacama hills, and highlighting the yellowish gardens and the old *Placilla Morales* peppertrees, a small grove in the middle of the most arid desert in the world, a square surrounded by a thick cast metal fence, a vestige of a glorious and exuberant past from the bonanza era of nitrate and the discovery of a grand silver deposit known as the *Mines of Chañarcillo.* These were the catalyst for an historic architectural flourishing of European art and culture in northern Chile, literally at the End of the World. It's hard to imagine the people of the XIX Century enjoying theatre plays and exquisite fine music from the cradle of Parisian and Italian art, making sense of the popular saying "There's nothing like the old days". And everything thanks to the economic opulence of mining and the settlement of European families, enticed by the riches of copper, silver and gold of northern Chile.

Esmeralda was rushing to work; she was driving her white dove, as her close ones called it, a flamboyant family Subaru car, when suddenly she was hit by a truck going at high speed, dragging her vehicle a few metres and pushing it off the side of the road. The truck driver didn't stop his lunatic race, continuing as if nothing had happened. With great effort, she was able to open the twisted door and get out of the car, apparently uninjured except that the strong impact had shaken her fragile body. With heavy breathing and a trembling voice, she placed her hands on her head and exclaimed:

–Oh God, oh God, I can't believe I just dodged that bullet! – She observed flabbergasted at how her white dove now looked, staring with dread and relief at the dents and chipped paint along the right side, tangible evidence of the strong impact; the bumper was torn off its anchor, the broken headlights and remains of the wing mirror lying in the middle of the road, scattered in a million pieces just a few metres behind, where it seemed that the truck driver had apparently lost control and caused the accident.

Esmeralda, known for her strong personality and facility to recover and react in extreme situations, took out her cell phone, called the insurance company and the police asking about the requirements and actions to follow. Since neither the engine nor the car's functioning were affected, she decided to get back on the road towards her office, first making a detour to the police station and the insurance company to make a statement about the accident.

At work, everyone was shocked about what had happened; some felt bad about the accident but were glad that it hadn't had major consequences. Meanwhile, a couple of women were gossiping and smoking a cigarette, while looking with obvious joy at the unfortunate accident; for them it was a reason to rejoice and they couldn't hide their satisfaction at the misfortune Esmeralda had suffered. On a daily basis, they felt exasperated by the joviality, joyfulness and spontaneity with which Esmeralda went about and lived her life, and by the physical and spiritual beauty she radiated. She wasn't aware of her privileged wealthy life, of her beauty, freedom, independence, and social status that allowed her access to a certain type of materialistic tranquillity and luxuries, such as wearing the latest fashion, showing off expensive jewellery, spending time with her friends at restaurants and bars, in addition to also travelling, thanks to her marvellous and magical red shoes, once or twice a year, to a different country and enjoying her holidays, happiness and independence that she had achieved after her divorce around three years ago, by daring to venture off alone, after realizing that she was missing the opportunity to travel because she had no one to do it with. Sometimes she would plan with some friend to go on holidays abroad, but in the end, they would always cancel, making her lose the opportunity to travel; she spent long weekends alone at home, but Pierina, the travel agency executive, helped her lose her fear and pushed her to travel on her own, just like her other clients had done as well.

She decided to make her first trip abroad alone for the holidays of September 18th, the date on which the anniversary of Chile's independence is celebrated, a week that she would supposedly enjoy with her children. However, two days before the trip, as she happily phoned them to organize some last minute details, she was hit by the surprising news that they wouldn't be able to go to the beach with her, because they would be spending the week of national holidays with their father. The news broke her, she was absolutely distraught, and she couldn't believe it, even though it was typical and not unexpected behaviour from her ex-husband. With a sad voice, she begged her children on the phone:

–Please, please, kids, let's go to the beach as we had planned, it's my turn to spend the holidays of 18th September with you all, last year it was with your father, this year it's my turn –she insisted as she broke down crying.

–Yeah mom, we know, but you know how dad is, if we leave him alone and go to the beach with you he's going to get mad, he'll be furious and will yell at us.

–This isn't fair, no, it isn't –she replied sobbing.

–Please, stop crying and being dramatic, mom, you both always put us in the middle of your fights. We have to go, mom –Renata hung up the phone.

That's how it's always been and still is up to this day, it's a love and fear relationship, he manipulates them, and they, out of fear or terror that he will punish them by denying certain economic privileges, do whatever he says, he's an expert in manipulating them and changing situations in his favour, he convinces them with his crocodile tears and whining, "your mother is the mean one, she left and abandoned you, and I, poor man, had to assume responsibility as father and mother", typical rosary that he repeated so much that even he believed it, forgetting that who had actually raised and taught the children was her. He was usually absent from home –-yes, he worked a lot, and nights and weekends he spent with his mistresses. When he did manage to stay home, life became a living hell with all the yelling and arguments, and plates flying in the air; he even grabbed and threw the Christmas tree one year; luckily the children were sleeping and didn't see all the commotion that could have tarnished the magic of Santa Claus and Christmas. Esmeralda always tried to keep her children from seeing or hearing their fights, although it was inevitable at times.

She remembered and had engraved into her mind and heart the memory of her psychology professor in one of the first classes she had attended as a university student, when he had spoken about the importance of the first years of life for the development and formation of the personality of each person, the fundamentals of having a good maternal and paternal image, and how in the absence of one of them, for example, of the father, it could be replaced by the father figure of a grandfather. She asked:

–What happens in the event that the father isn't a good person, for example, is a delinquent or is aggressive towards the mother?

The professor replied in a reflective tone:

–Esteemed students, regardless of how their parents are, children need a father and mother figure for their integral formation.

Esmeralda always remembered that first psychology class, making it her own and practicing it on a daily basis in her role as a mother. Despite the disagreements between them, Esmeralda tried to be a good example for her three children, she at least tried; their father, on the contrary, acted differently undermining and belittling her role as a mother, which he constantly repeated to his children. In addition to Esmeralda's sadness, bitterness, nervousness and irritability in which she found herself, the atmosphere at home became thicker and gloomy, the children saw a grumpy mother and a happy father, playful, who let them do whatever they pleased, constantly undermining their mothers' orders, amen to financial power.

When they turned 15, he gifted them with a car. Yes, it was a great gift that the children anxiously waited for. It was absurd and extremely irresponsible, as they were not yet old enough to get a driver's license, which is obtained from the age of seventeen after passing a written and practical test, in addition to always having to drive accompanied by an adult.

In that duality between teachings and gifts, it was very easy for a young adolescent to decide where to go, and the case of Esmeralda's children was not an exception. There were several accidents, fortunately without mishap other than vehicular damages and the great fright experienced by the children. With his influential power, with just a single phone call the police procedures that were taking place would magically be called off, and the police would quickly leave the scene and even apologize, after receiving a phone call from one of their higher-ranking superiors.

Esmeralda lived between two worlds – on the one hand, with a public image of a lucky woman and happy wife to the manager of a well-known mining company, enjoying all the comforts and luxuries which that implied, and on the other hand, a second life inside of a majestic mansion of more than twenty-five rooms, with en-suite bedrooms and even with a jacuzzi in most of them, gardens, a pool with a waterfall and service rooms. However, she wasn't happy in her home, being abused daily just for being a woman, mother and wife, who overlooked every violent outburst. She was overpowered, mistreated and undermined. The mistreatment was evident from the time they were dating, in her young university years; she forgave him every time and let each violent situation go with ease. It was so easy for her to forgive and forget because she was deeply in love.

The most violent moment in her relationship, when she truly noticed what awaited her, was her wedding day. It turns out that her closest and dearest cousin had travelled from Santiago to Concepción, a long ten hours trip by bus with her boyfriend, her mother, despite her disapproval, they had managed to see each other and continue with their relationship. The invitation to the wedding was a great opportunity for them to share and enjoy their love, that was why after the religious ceremony and at the party, Patricia approached Esmeralda and, in a whisper, asked:

–Cousin, everything is splendid, however, we are pretty exhausted from the trip and need to rest. Can we go to your apartment and sleep for a couple of hours?

–Yes, of course cousin, Esmeralda replied, understanding the situation as she stood up to find the keys; she walked them out and gave them directions, and as she was coming back, in the middle of the darkness she spotted Mario, who was approaching her with a steady step. With an expression of concern and curiosity he asked:

–Where are you coming from? and he added with a frown: where did you go? You left the party without even telling me.

–I went to show my cousin how to get to the apartment; they left to rest because they were exhausted from the tremendous trip, they took so they could be here with us at our wedding.

–What? Are you telling me that you gave them the keys to our apartment? And they plan on sleeping in our bed? –he began to yell, furious, his face disfigured and outraged.

–Yes, yes, but what's wrong with that? Esmeralda wanted to know.

–How dare you give them the keys to the apartment, are you crazy? that pair of … only want to have sex and you're condoning it, and raising his hand he slapped her across the face:

–Paff!!!

Esmeralda was blown away, in shock; she couldn't believe what she was going through on the day of her wedding and just a few hours after celebrating her religious marriage ceremony. He immediately hugged her apologizing for having slapped her, adding in a plaintive tone:

I never meant to hit you, but you drive me crazy, as he kept hugging her tightly against his chest.

After a few minutes, they returned to the party. As they were seen entering the room, Esmeralda's father exclaimed: Look, here come the love birds, we were starting to miss you, come here my friends and raising his glass with glee he added: Let's make another toast to the newlyweds!

Esmeralda marries wearing strictly black in her first marriage

Mario wouldn't leave her alone, he held her by his side as if wanting to protect her, but at the same time preventing her from telling any of the guests what had just occurred. She kept silent, with obvious signs of tiredness and sleepiness. However, what really kept her in that state of stillness was the shock caused by the slap, received from whom was her husband and father of the child she was expecting. She couldn't put words together, even less ask someone for help. Here is another trait to keep in mind, fear of what our parents will think, to their teachings and worrying about what they and others will say: she felt that she couldn't ruin the party and even less be ungrateful towards the guests, so she pulled herself together the best way she could and acted as though "nothing had happened here".

She missed a great opportunity to break the cycle of domestic violence that awaited her; it would have been better to reach out to her father, sisters, even to her cousin, and her friends. But it was not to be, she didn't enjoy that kind of trust and no way would she have been willing to cause misery to her guests, and even less to her father.

Years went by, and with them the escalation of violence, usually caused by jealousy hallucinations; he was always looking, snooping and doubting, with an unreasonable and out of control distrust towards Esmeralda and without motive. Never did she once think about or look at another man, but as the saying goes "he who has done it will suspect it". The infidelities became part of everyday life, and with them the recurrent visits to the gynaecologist. Esmeralda suffered too much because of those infidelities and domestic violence, she cried a lot, she was too thin, nervous and irritable.

One Sunday morning something very special occurred. She was lying in bed when she burst into tears, she could no longer bear the pain that stifled her, she knew that he was with his mistress and it was something she couldn't stand nor take anymore; she was sobbing inconsolably when her cry was suddenly interrupted by a tiny pair of hands trying to shake her and a very soft voice, mixed with amazement and sorrow, whispered to her; it was her daughter Victoria, barely 5 years old:

–Mummy, mummy, don't cry, mummies don't cry.

–Wow! It was shocking to hear her daughter say that mothers don't cry, that forced her to be more careful and prevent her children from ever seeing her suffer again and even less cry. That perhaps was the start of a self-imposed prohibition against crying, because with time it became harder for her to shed a tear; even though the pain was killing her inside, she couldn't cry. It may have been a self-defence and a protection mechanism she had unconsciously developed to safeguard her children.

But when she does manage to cry it's due to extreme pain, she can't control it, she can cry for days, long endless nights, not eating and locking herself absorbed in thoughts from which no one could pull her out, not even herself, until she would shed the very last tear left inside her body.

Mario knew and was aware of what she did, in more than one occasion (at such moments when weakness or remorse weighed on his mind) he revealed himself to be sweet, showing signs of true regret and even innocence:

–Esmi, you are a very noble woman and I've been so cruel to you; you could have cheated on me with whoever you wanted and as many times as you wished, and I bet that hasn't even crossed your mind. How could you think that! she exclaimed, adding: of course not, I would never do that because I am your wife. Or do you believe that I am a bad woman? she asked in a tone of wanting to know his opinion.

She was so insecure! After marrying she lost her sparkle, her joy, her energy, her confidence and self-esteem, love and passion for great challenges and dreams, such as making the decision to go to university and study, without precedent in her family, being the only one of the six siblings to have done it, and by her own means, efforts and abilities, leaving the countryside in search of a new life through a professional career.

Mario had crushed, annihilated and trample on her defiant personality. The certainty of knowing she could do whatever she set her mind to was now part of the past, she had low self-esteem and was no longer acting like herself, cheerful, independent and sure of herself. Living in a marriage filled with misunderstandings, can completely change the life of a woman and also of a man, although fortunately for men they are less affected by it. How different life would have been for Esmeralda and her children if her marriage hadn't been an unsuitable one; they had everything they needed to be happy and proud as a family. She loved him deeply, they both had university degrees, excellent jobs and a bright future ahead of them, but no, money and misogyny and believing he owned the world destroyed it all, to the point that Esmeralda was on the brink of losing her life owing to the high degree of physical domestic violence, and because of the sadness and depression she was submerged in that drove her to attempt suicide.

Luckily and ironically, there are dramatic events that flick a switch in some people's minds managing to wake them up, to come out and cry for help as they realize they were born to be happy and not to suffer, that the world is a wonderful place and that there are a million reasons to live and be happy, starting with loving themselves, holding on to that little bit of self-love and the urge to keep living that is left, which in reality is a lot.

With the support from her mother, friendships related to her children's school and her closeness with the Catholic Church, she clung to life and to a three year psychiatric treatment, with which she managed to be reborn just like a phoenix, regaining her excitement to live, to be happy, to have fun, to work, to make a name for herself professionally, to dress and wear makeup to her liking, to let her hair grow out, to wear tight clothes if she felt like it, to go out for coffee with girlfriends without being treated like a bad woman, and to start trusting the opposite sex, realizing that not all men are bad or sick.

She was left with one great pain in her heart: not having been able to have a beautiful family and give her beloved children a home filled with love, security and happiness. It's the karma that will follow her for the rest of her life, without losing hope of maybe one day regaining her confidence and building a healthy relationship of love and respect with her children.

She survived domestic violence and the loss of her three children, who chose to stay with their father, after they had permanently separated, although they were already teenagers, and even Apollo was starting his first year of university, in addition to overcoming the grief after her separation, because in those times civil divorce didn't yet exist in Chile, only annulments, an unthinkable choice for her owing to the impossibility of reaching an agreement with Mario, besides the fact that he boasted that he would never get divorced, being the perfect excuse for not have to marry any of his mistresses. However, as soon as the Divorce Law was passed in Chile, Esmeralda hired a prestigious lawyer who in ~~no~~ time successfully filed for divorce, regaining like that her long-awaited freedom. It was so exhausting and in poor taste that every time she had to do important paperwork, she had to give information as a married woman and, therefore, she was giving her ex-husband's information, of whom she didn't even have the address. It was a true nightmare. Regaining her freedom and independence completely changed her life, and that was the last stepping stone in her therapy, although the relationship and reconciliation with her children remained pending to be able to achieve happiness, tranquillity and peace of mind for her and her kids.

Returning to the traumatic fact that she couldn't enjoy her children's company during the week of the national holidays, she decided, drawing strength from her weakness, to consult the travel agency and follow with strong conviction the advice that the executive woman had given her, who urged her to travel alone.

–Pierina, Pierina, please, send me anywhere on holidays, I can't stay here alone in Copiapó, everyone will go sightseeing and to the beach –adding–: I asked for time off so I could go on holidays with my children but they ended up choosing, as usual, their father, please give me an all-inclusive package to the Caribbean for the whole week.

–Ok, where do you want to go?

–Anywhere, I just want to get out of Copiapó, I don't want to be here during the national holidays locked up and crying.

–Let me see and I'll let you know. What do you think about San Andrés, Colombia, or Isla del Carmen, México? Cartagena, Colombia?

–Anywhere, now I have to get back to the office.

That is how Esmeralda learned to make use of her resilience to overcome every lash her ex-husband kept giving her despite being separated. Pierina called her very concerned, commenting that there were no tickets and hotels available to the touristic places she had mentioned, but Rio de Janeiro, Brazil, was a possibility and also Buenos Aires, Argentina. Esmeralda energetically replied:

–No, thank you, I've been to those countries many times before, please keep looking".

–But tell me what else is available, because I don't know where else to look.

–The Bahamas, French West Indies, or Punta Cana again.

At the end of the day, she received another phone call from the executive woman, who informed her that she had not been able to find anything, that there was only one possibility and that could be Montego Bay, Jamaica.

–Jamaica?! Wow, fantastic! Send me to Jamaica, it's a country I've always wanted to visit, that's awesome, I'm so happy, excited.

–Yes, Ms. Esmeralda, there is a "but" though, actually two, it is really expensive, twice the price of Brazil, Argentina and Colombia, and with a stop of eight hours in Miami.

–What? Eight hours in Miami! Do you expect me to spend eight hours of my holidays stuck in an airport? No, impossible, thank you.

–Then there's nothing I can do, I'm sorry.

–What do you mean I'm sorry? I haven't given up just yet, explain to me what the stop in Miami implies. Can I take another flight, for example, the next day?

–Yes, of course, and they respect the price, because it would be on the same itinerary, only on a different date.

–Ok, case closed, as doctor Polo would say. Keep me two days in Miami, I'd rather walk around Florida than waste eight hours of my trip at the airport –she exclaimed with a sigh of joy and smiling as she left the travel agency, happier than the three little pigs.

She was organizing her luggage when she remembered she had cousins living in Miami, whom she hadn't seen since childhood, more than twenty years ago (well, easily thirty years ago), when her aunt and uncle decided to move to Isla Margarita, Venezuela; later they separated and in the face of the political and financial crisis product of the *Chavismo*, the cousins moved to the United States in search of a better life and safety. She called her mother to see if she had either a phone number or any information she could use to get in contact with her cousins.

–No, I don't have anything, but I can get it for you.

–Ah, really? Thank you so much.

For Esmeralda's mother, as well as for her, everything was possible and they were really good, resourceful and diligent at getting information and solving problems. That was surely how she managed to get her cousin George to pick her up from the airport and spent a wonderful and unforgettable weekend with her beloved cousins; they had a fabulous time remembering anecdotes from their childhood and touring the bay on a yacht, she was welcomed and treated like a princess, to the point that they didn't want her to continue her trip to Jamaica, they asked her to stay with them, but no, she followed her itinerary as planned.

When she arrived in Montego Bay, she found that the hotel was of great luxury, a resort of innumerable buildings, gardens, and swimming pools by the ocean.

The room she was assigned to was on the ground floor, in a corner, and it opened on to a small patio with a skylight. The bedroom was beautiful, with all types of amenities, including a jacuzzi. But the warm air in Jamaica was too hot for her, causing her to breathe heavily as though she were short of breath; without feeling comfortable, she took a deep breath and went to the front desk. With a very friendly, smiling and flattering way, greeted the receptionist trying to win his approval and get what she needed.

–My dear sir, I'm so happy to be in your country, and even though it's late and dark I can appreciate the beauty and charm of its land, and especially its people.

–Thank you very much, pretty lady, that's Jamaica, beautiful, and tomorrow you will see the beauty of its beaches, palm trees, gardens and all the amenities of our resort, which is five stars.

–Yes, everything is wonderful, however, I have a major…major…problem –she was abruptly interrupted by the concierge, who stretched out his arm with his hand facing Esmeralda like a stop sign, at the same time that with the other hand he placed his index finger on his lips indicating silence, exclaiming with concern:

–Shh, shh, please, no, you can't say that, you cannot say that word –now it is her who interrupts him with a questioning surprised look on her face wanting to understand what was wrong with what she was trying to say:

–But how, if I have a problem? –Once again, she received the same reaction–: Shhhh!

–No, that's not how you say it, you have to say "I have a situation", it sounds more elegant and it drives away bad energy.

–Mmm, I understand, only "peace and love" –she made the peace sign with her fingers followed by the gesture of smoking weed. Sighing she commented:

–Mmmm, I understand, I understand, no problem, sorry, sorry, I just remembered Bob Marley, that's how he sings, right?

–That's right, my pretty young lady, you're supposed to say "I have a situation", tell me what is the situation that's bothering you, because here we are at your service and to make you feel comfortable and happy, so that you may enjoy your stay and holiday.

–It turns out that the room I was assigned to is quite lovely, comfortable and cosy, but it doesn't have a view of the ocean, not even of the pool, I suffer from anxiety and claustrophobia –adding in a flirtatious tone like a spoiled little girl, those girls that get everything they want thanks to their charm –by being alone I'll have no one to protect me, I'll feel like I'm suffocating and I'll likely have an anxiety attack in such an enclosed room.

–Mmm, I understand your situation.

–Please, would you be kind enough to see if there's a possibility that I could switch rooms? Ideally on the second or third floor, with an ocean view, or at least overlooking the pool, would it be possible?

–Let me see…let me see…what we have to offer you.

She was looking at him with an angelic face and very flirtatious, like a spoiled little girl.

–Let me tell you that in addition to being very beautiful, you are a very lucky lady, we have one available room on the second floor, and it's even larger, with a spectacular view of the gardens.

Esmeralda responded with evident discontent and trying to get something better:

–But, what about another room with an ocean view?

–Let me finish, do not be impatient, the room that I'm offering you is number 17, with a view of the gardens, pool and the beach!

–Wow! Amazing! You've outdone yourself! That's awesome! Thank you, thank you very much! –and throwing herself over the counter, she hugged him and planted a huge kiss on his cheek. She couldn't be happier, she radiated so much joy.

The next morning, the warmth and tropical humidity characteristic of the Caribbean, together with the clarity of the day, the singing of birds and sounds of waterfalls flowing from one pool to the other, said good morning. Dazzled by the intensity of the sun and the majesty of the scene in front of her, she was absolutely perplexed when she opened the curtains of her room window that went from wall to wall; her gaze was lost in the immensity of the ocean, the palm trees on the beach shore, the beauty of the gardens with an aromatic tropical fragrance and the immense swimming pools. That was just a small part of the exuberant beauty of the scenery. She quickly showered and got ready for breakfast, and as she passed by the front desk she was greeted very warmly and invited to a welcome gathering, after enjoying an exquisite and abundant breakfast consisting of fruits, omelette and fresh juice. She greeted each person who crossed her path and she began to make herself known and to make friends; the restaurant staff gave her detailed information on the benefits and amenities of the resort.

View from the resort room

As always, her way of holidaying was to enjoy the infrastructure and amenities of the resort during the first day, ask about nearby tours and learn a little more about the area. By getting acquainted at the front desk, she was able to benefit by booking a couple of tours, one to do a kind of safari through the jungle, including hikes and canopy descents and the other to go to the seven rivers and a yacht trip. In one of the adjoining buildings there were nightclubs (it was one of the services offered by the resort), where everything was included, even cigarettes and cigars; the most pleasant thing was the transfer service in golf carts, by reserving the departure and return time, although the return time could vary, because you never knew what you could find and what the night could be like.

They called her room letting her know that her transportation was ready, and what chivalry the driver had in opening the door so she could get in and take her to the other end of the building – about five minutes away –. Nights at the club were so much fun, with tourists from all over the world and in the mood to have a good time, it was like being in paradise. She was really enjoying herself; it was the pleasure of drinking whatever she wanted without being worried about the cost or the currency exchange, it was a perfect holiday. And talking about money, that day when she needed it to pay for the tours, she noticed that she didn't have her wallet nor her documents with her, she had lost them; she went through all her luggage until she remembered that the night before, as she arrived to her assigned room, before going to the front desk, she had left them under her pillow. She immediately went to the front desk, luckily finding herself with the same staff from the night before. After kindly greeting them, she said in a serious tone:

–I have a situation.

–Tell us what happened, what is your situation?

–I've lost my wallet with all my documents, credit cards and money.

–No, no, it can't be, how? Surely there must be a mistake. Did you look thoroughly through your things?

–Yes, I already did and I couldn't find it, I think it's in the room that I was assigned to yesterday.

–Oh, no, it can't be, because more guests arrived and they haven't said anything and neither has the maid– he commented with great concern and in disbelief, while he checked in a big book and on the computer, until suddenly, looking at the computer screen, he exclaimed with joy and surprise:

–Ah, no, that room is still unoccupied! Although it's strange that the maid didn't turn anything in to the front desk this morning after cleaning the rooms, how odd, something here isn't right – commenting as he came out from behind the counter, and approaching Esmeralda, he offered her his arm and charmingly said–: Come, my pretty lady, let's go check the room.

And they went walking through the corridors in lively conversation, like great friends. Esmeralda was one of a kind, with an incredible ability to make friends and share with everyone. He opened the room door and she strode towards the bed, lifting the covers and pillow, took the wallet and exclaimed with great relief and joy:

–See, my wallet was here, just where I had left it, under the pillow, no problem, sorry, sorry, all is good, thank you very much – and she ran to give him a huge hug and a kiss, just like she had done the night before when he had managed to switch her room.

It was an incredible holiday, by far one of the best; despite having travelled alone, she never felt abandoned and even less sad, she was always surrounded by many people, sharing with other tourists and the resort staff, who were very friendly and always willing to provide any service she required. The tours she booked were a real pleasure and an adventure and she enjoyed them to the fullest; the Rastafari and canopy tour being so unique and incredible, beginning at midmorning. They picked her up in a van, and together with other tourists they embarked until they reached the tourism agency, where a tour guide was waiting for them and who invited them to hop on a military-type truck, the roof covered with a tarp and provided with a pair of rustic wooden benches on each side; around a dozen tourists were seated, it was extremely hot and the atmosphere was suffocating from the humidity. When they got off the truck, a couple of tour guides were waiting for them, after giving them the instructions and recommendations, they handed them the equipment. They walked through narrow paths ascending until they reached a certain point where there was a type of cage or large basket, where the canopy line began. The first to climb was one of the tour guides, who released a Tarzan type of scream and began the journey, stopping at about a hundred and fifty meters away where there was another cage, and under it and everyone's feet there was an endless precipice; however, thanks to the thickness of the jungle they could enjoy the adrenaline without being aware of what height they were, and thus they enjoyed the journey, some more scared than others, supporting and encouraging each other with the conviction that they wanted to live this adventure.

Esmeralda was fascinated by it all, she had always liked strong emotions and extreme sports; she rapidly glided through the line until she reached the second stop where she had to descend in free fall. It was an extraordinary rush of emotion; she remembered how fire-fighters quickly slide down the iron pole to get to the fire truck. It was a wonderful day, despite all the mosquito bites on her arms and legs. That night she enjoyed the nightclub even more after making new friends with whom to share and talk about the events of the day.

The next day there was another great adventure, an excursion. They passed through secret waterfalls until they reached the house where the legendary reggae singer Bob Marley had lived. That is an experience that she always remembers with great amusement: she took a double tour to Negril Beach and a catamaran cruise, and the fun part about it was that in the middle of the ocean in full party mode, with a few rum and colas in the body, dancing to the rhythm of reggae and enjoying the tropical rain that fell every so often, everyone in their bathing suits, a smiling young Jamaican man was walking around with lotion in his hands, approaching tourists even though he was not welcome, until he walked up to Esmeralda offering her a massage, to which she flatly refused with a smile:

–No, thank you, I don't like massages.

–That's because you've never tried my massages, you'll love them. Come, you won't regret it.

–No, thank you.

–Come on –the Jamaican man insisted–, it'll only be on your feet.

– Ah, yeah? Ok, in that case go ahead.

It was a lot of fun; she couldn't stop laughing; she was so ticklish on the soles of her feet that it was more of a laughter therapy session than a massage session.

Her trip to Jamaica was a wakeup call in her life,

and the rediscovery of happiness

A foot massage by a young Jamaican man

Another of her fun experiences was standing under the waterfalls that joined together with the seabed, just like those sexy calendar girls.

Those were days of fulfilment, amusement and fun. She enjoyed them like a child, radiating light, energy and happiness. She was loved by everyone; she never had dinner or breakfast alone. Ah! There was a prank that the lifeguards liked to play, apparently it was forbidden to dive into the pool, and she had liked diving ever since she was a little girl, competing with her siblings to see who could jump in the farthest, who could hold their breath the longest, mocking and laughing out loud at whoever landed in a belly flop. She used to sit near one of the lifeguards to sunbathe, feeling more protected and secure with her belongings by leaving them under his care while she walked on the beach or went swimming in the ocean, or had a drink under the palm trees on the beach shore, she loved drinking piña colada at the bar inside the pool, sitting on the cement floor with the water at waist level was amazing, as well as moving across the pool with a glass in her hand sharing with other swimmers, women, children and men, with everyone, she was extremely sociable and friendly, being liked by everyone. After flipping through a magazine and brochures that offered tours and, enjoying the marvellous weather and sun for almost an hour, she decided to go for a swim, and naturally and as she was accustomed to do at her swimming pool at home, she dived into the water. Suddenly she heard the sound of the lifeguard's whistle, scared and worried she wanted to know what was happening, what was the emergency (saddened that it was an emergency and that someone could be drowning). The lifeguard gave her an inquisitive look gesturing with his hand for her to approach him:

–Diving in the pool isn't allowed, –he informed her: please do not do it again he said in a soft and firm tone.

–But why if I'm on holidays? When one is on holidays they can do as they pleased, right? –she responded, hoping for an affirmative reply.

–I'm sorry miss, here it is forbidden because it is dangerous, you could fall in the wrong way and hurt yourself, besides disturbing other tourists as you splash water, he said very kindly.

–I understand, I'm sorry, she replied like a little girl, sinking and hiding herself so as not to show the embarrassment shown by her face.

However, Esmeralda was known to be very mischievous, spontaneous and playful, she didn't always obey warnings and recommendations, even less if it was about having a good time, and thus every day she managed to evade the sight of the lifeguards and dive into the pool. They kindly greeted each other and talked about the beauty of Jamaica, its beaches and the resort's amenities, among other topics, until she would say something random to them to distract their attention, for example, she asked him with a surprised look on her face as she got up from the beach chair:

–Look, the man that's coming over, is he your boss? –And as soon as he turned to look, she had already dived into the pool and from afar looking at him and laughing out loud. And she came up with something every day, or took advantage of the moments where they would walk around the pool or talked with other tourist or even talked on the radio, the thing is that it was sacred for her to dive into the pool every day, just as she enjoyed swimming towards the buoys in the ocean.

That's how she became known and loved by everyone, at the bar, at the pool, at the beach, at the nightclub and by the entertainment team, where she participated everyday encouraging and supporting the integration of children and adults. On the last day of her holiday, she was having such a great time that she didn't want to miss a minute of it, she had lunch and went to enjoy the pool before the taxi picked her up to take her to the airport. She was happily swimming, as if time was not pressing, when she heard a woman's voice with whom she had been sharing days before:

–Esmi, Esmi, doesn't your flight leave today? What are you still doing in the pool?

–Yes, I leave today, but I still have time to swim and enjoy my holidays

–Noooo, look at the time, let's go, get out of the water, it's time or you'll miss your flight.

Smiling she responded:

–Just a little longer, just a little longer –and she continued to repeatedly dive into the water ignoring the advice, and kept swimming and playing in the water just like a child whose parents have to call over and over again to get out of the pool, but who just wants to keep playing. Several people who noticed she was still in the pool and were aware that the time of her flight was approaching, showed her their watch and warned her that she would miss her flight if she didn't hurry, to the point that an echo was heard coming from everywhere:

–Esmeraldaaaa, Esmeraldaaaa, it's time for you to get out of the pool.

–Esmi, it's time for you to get ready, they're coming to pick you up to take you to the airport.

–Get out of the water, child, it's time for your flight, or do you wish to stay?

–Ah! It looks like she doesn't want to go back home.

Like a mermaid, she dove and swam underwater, not wanting to hear what everyone had to say and wishing time would stop, until she finally emerged from the water, everyone saying "Bye, have a nice trip, it was a pleasure getting to know you and sharing with you, we will miss you, write, call, don't lose my phone number nor my email address."

She left jumping, singing and smiling… It was the beginning of a custom she would acquire of travelling and holidaying alone, in reality the only thing she did alone was to travel, she enjoyed the company of everyone at airports, hotels, resorts, tours, and anywhere she could possibly be.

Her trip to Jamaica was the awakening to her true personality and way of being, of a happy, spontaneous, sociable, confident woman, trusting in others, without fear or prejudice; she was an adult child, a chance to wear her brand new marvellous and magical little red shoes. Shoes that would take her to explore and enjoy places she would have never imagined, like the pyramids of Giza in Egypt, the papyri in Cairo and Sharm El Sheikh with a tour that included a camel ride and stargazing in the Sharm desert, where she had to spend the night in the middle of the pampas after the bus had left without her and her friend Keith; Italy with its beautiful Venice, Naples and Tuscany; Turkey with its mosque and the Grand Bazaar in Istanbul; Paris, with its museums and art; Germany, highlighting the visit to Hansel and Gretel's house; and much of old Great Britain, including the land of whisky such as Edinburgh, Scotland, and the university cities of Oxford and Cambridge; and in South America she would visit places such as Colombia and its city of San Andrés, Puerto Rico, Mexico, Costa Rica, the Dominican Republic, and Rio de Janeiro in Brazil where she would venture the longest as the pilgrim bride.

Her life was financially stable and comfortable; she had several properties, including a beautiful summer beach house, in one of the most attractive and touristic cities of northern Chile known as Bahía Inglesa. Of course she wasn't aware of the privilege and of the financial comforts in which she lived, in her almost 20 years of her marriage with the father of her children, who thanks to his engineering studies had accepted the position of manager at a large mining company, –a position that he held for more than 20 years and had quit just one year before the accident–, which in the future would be known worldwide due to the Copiapó mining accident, caused by the collapse of the San Jose mine, a major accident that occurred Thursday, August 5th, 2010 around 2:30 p.m., leaving 33 miners trapped at a depth of 729 meters underground for about 69 days. On Sunday, August 22nd, 17 days after the accident, the miners were found alive, managing to be successfully rescued on October 22nd, thanks to the excellent work of the government and the international support, by drilling escape boreholes to transport them to the surface in rescue capsules dubbed Phoenix. On Wednesday, October 13th, 2010, and ten minutes past midnight, they were able to retrieve the first miner to the surface, continuing with the rest at a rate of about one per hour. Till this day, it has been the largest and most successful rescue in the history of mining worldwide, being the event with the largest media coverage of those characteristics with about 1,000 to 1,300 million viewers.

Esmeralda was aware of the risk that entailed working in the San Jose mine, it was common for her husband to tell her about the frequent accidents that occurred, many of them being handled privately to avoid paying high premiums, and more than that, suspension or closure of the mining operation by the competent body. She remembers that once a week, Mario had to inspect the work that was done inside the mine, and on the morning of that day, he looked at her with extreme concern and fear:

–Esmi, my love, today I have to go down to the mine, I don't know if I'll make it out of that hellhole alive –he said as he hugged her tightly, as if looking for contention and at the same time silently saying goodbye, saying to himself–: I'm not going to die, I can't die, God is with me, he won't let me down.

–I love you Esmi, please, if I don't make it out alive from the mine, take care of our children. If I die, they'll be financially settled for life, you won't have to worry about that, they won't lack anything; my contract stipulates any event and the indemnification is worth millions, so don't you worry about it.

–Please...please...don't go to the mine, don't go down there, you're the manager, it's not necessary that you go down there, you give the orders, please...please...–she begged him with tears in her eyes.

–That's the job, my love, even more so being the boss, I need to go down to the mine to see the boreholes and the lode trails, as well as to cheer the oldies up –that's what they are called in mining jargon, and in general referring nicely and respectfully to workers who perform tough jobs of great physical wear and of construction.

–But why don't they do something to fortify the tunnels and prevent further collapses and slabs from occurring. It's terrible, those workers can't continue to get injured and even less die from being crushed by the landslides and slabs that often occur in that mine.

–Yes, fortification work is done, but it's impossible and expensive to fortify the entire mine, besides remember that the owners are cheap and stingy, although they've been really generous with me –and he added–: there are kilometres and kilometres long tunnels, impossible to coat and fortify everything, it is impossible, what more would we want than to work peacefully and continue to produce without having an oldie getting injured.

–But, why not close that mine and work in another? –Esmeralda insisted with a concerned tone and in search of answers and solutions.

–Yes, we are looking for another mining field; let's hope that the moles (mining jargon for miners), our topographers and geologists do well, so we can start working in a new mine and forget about this hellhole. However, for the time being we must continue working and producing. I have to go now, wish me luck Mario replied as he grabbed the keys and wallet that were on the nightstand of their master bedroom.

–Yes, my dear, I will pray for you that nothing bad happens at the mine, please, be very careful and try to avoid entering the mine, Esmeralda begged.

–Enough, shut up, I already told you I have to do it, I have to go down to the mine, it's my responsibility and my job, don't make things more difficult, Mario snapped raising his voice and with an evident tone of anger, as he walked away through the long corridor that led to the entrance hall of their immense and beautiful home.

That's the life of a miner's family, uncertain and living in permanent terror, not just the families of the mine workers themselves or field workers, it is a large group of people that when an accident occurs, everyone in the company is affected in one way or another, they can even lose their job if the mining site was to close, as it happened in the San José mine.

The mining job allowed her, coming as she did from a lower-middle class family, to access in a meteoric way a comfortable and luxurious life, one that would have been unthinkable for her parents but one that her grandparents had enjoyed due to a bonanza in the rapid development of agriculture in the early 1900s and before the agrarian reform. This had been thanks to the great visionary work of grandfather Ismael, who had inherited and acquired large agricultural lands, successfully cultivating them with the acquisition and use of the first agricultural machinery that had arrived in the country in those years, making a small fortune that allowed him the pleasure of buying a considerable number of houses in the countryside and in the capital of Chile, Santiago; his tradition was to pass down a house to each of his seven children at the moment of marriage, facilitating the start of their own family and giving them financial security.

That is how thanks to the great economic solvency, full of material comforts, with pleasure trips abroad and his children attending the best school in Copiapó with a prestigious reputation, exclusive education and dominance of the English language, teachings that had begun to be desired and necessary. The San Lorenzo School was built as an exclusive and elite educational establishment, with the strategy to attract the families of executives from transnational mining companies, providing a great quality of education for their children, making it possible to transfer American families to a zone with an arid climate, without vegetation or technological advances. However, what usually happens is that families who arrive to the North of Chile end up falling in love with the weather, the wonderful beaches, valleys and colourful hills, the mountain range with its lakes and highland fauna. Nevertheless, it wasn't very desirable to move North, at least in those years, because of the distance from the large urban areas and therefore devoid of the comforts they were accustomed to in their home country, even basic and vital services such as access to quality education and health, and most of all without entertainment shows, reasons why the company was known for the development of art and culture, leading and organizing events of outstanding artistic and musical quality, theatre plays and exhibitions for the benefit of the mining elite and the associated companies and the rich families and socialites from Copiapó, whom, as well as having a refined taste and purchasing power, this made it possible for them to make new friendships, opening horizons for great opportunities, especially for their children.

In short, it was a life of "Bilz and Paps", referring to the name of two Chilean soft drinks with their slogan "I want a different world", where Bilz and Paps invited their consumers to live a world full of entertainment and fantasy with their funny characters Bily and Maik. That's how it was, and it was even very common for them to receive jokes about it, with frequent pleasure trips to the majestic South of the national territory and fall in love with the area of Villarrica and Pucón with its beautiful greenery, lakes, waterfalls, ancient forests, hot springs and the intrepid Trancura River, where they enjoyed with high adrenaline the sailing down its torrential waters and steep rapids. One summer they were placidly walking at sunset visiting the tourist shops and artisanal fairs when they were stopped by the typical young guy with a good physique and a very cheerful, sparkling appearance, offering them the experience of Tandem skydiving. Esmeralda, with her passion for living adrenaline high experiences, asked:

–Tell me, tell me, what is it about, I'm really interested in it, let me see…let me see…

–Please, come, come to our travel agency so we can show you videos and photos.

Everyone was fascinated except for Mario, he wasn't a risk taker and was always worried that something could happen at not allowing both of them to be present, risking suffering harm, because one of them had to stay alive to take care of the children. So, she embarked herself on the adventure that provided a 100 per cent adrenaline rush. Apollo and Victoria accompanied her on the plane ride to watch the jump, she couldn't ignore the fact that despite her great enthusiasm and full conviction to jump, it was inevitable to feel fear. She remembers that when the pilot told the instructor they had reached the ideal altitude to jump, her heart began to beat so fast that she felt like she was going to die, and for a couple of seconds she even hesitated whether to jump or not. The instructor was an expert at convincing tourists and he wasn't going to let the client escape at that stage of the adventure and with both of her kids looking at her, no, no, obviously it wouldn't be a dignified attitude and under no circumstance could she embarrass herself, so she gathered courage like a good Chilean woman and said "OK", getting into the pre-jump position as she was taught, trying to hold on with her right hand to one of the sides of the tiny door, the speed of the wind fiercely pushed her arm to the other side. The instructor helped her get into position and yelled:

–Hold on tight, on the count of three we will jump! –Showing his fingers–: one…two…three!!

–What an incredible experience! It was a spectacular sensation, divine, compared to one of those orgasms that make you moan with pleasure and sweat from head to toe. That minute in free fall reminded her of *Juan Salvador Gaviota* and let her body go in total freedom surrendering to the adventure and the daring turns she made with the instructor, opening arms and legs in a cross, turning from side to side and even doing front flips …a once in a lifetime experience… The following day she did it again, and during the next summers, it wasn't just one or two jumps, they were many more and accompanied by Apollo and Victoria, who also dared to jump. Renata couldn't do it, due to her young age and short height, she couldn't live the experience. It was the beginning of skydiving for Esmeralda, a hobby she practiced every time she had the chance. Ah, in Esmeralda's first jump, Apollo and Victoria, were surprised experiencing the G-force on the way back after their mother's jump, the pilot did it very quickly and abruptly, making them feel like their face was disfigured by the change in atmospheric pressure, a fact they related with great euphoria and adrenaline, once in a science class, when the teacher tried to explain what the G-force was, Apollo raised his hand and explained to his classmates in great detail what it was about, thus earning a good grade and an extra point for the next exam.

Esmeralda recommended it to her most daring friends and adrenaline lovers, like herself, to practice tandem and skydiving, taking the time to explain with real passion what it was to live the experience of tandem jumping, her eyes twinkled and she moved her hands reliving her experiences and explaining in great detail:

–Tandem is a free fall, it's an activity that lets you discover skydiving in a fast and safe way by jumping with a qualified instructor, who has total control of the jump, all you have to do is enjoy the ride. They give you a 15 minutes talk explaining the instructions, they put you on a plane equipped with the appropriate suit and ready to jump, the flight is very pleasant, you fly over Lake Villarrica and you pass through the volcano slopes of the same name, with an exceptional view of the most beautiful natural landscapes in Latin America. The free fall lasts less than a minute at 200 kilometres per hour, and at 1,500 meters of altitude the instructor opens the parachute, at that height you enjoy the flight for about 5 to 10 minutes before landing on the beach of Lake Villarrica, adding: "you should have seen how tourists and people in the water started screaming in terror when they saw us approaching the beach. You can't miss it the next time you go on holidays to Pucón. If you want, I can come with you, I volunteer to jump with you, since I'm already an expert.

Those first few seconds enjoying the free fall were the beginning of her love and passion for skydiving, with the parachute still closed, she loved moving her body left and right. It was so pleasant and mind-blowing, comparable only to the most outrageous, sweaty, exhilarating orgasm she had had at the height of the years of fiery sexuality and exorbitant youth. They were dreamed family holidays, longed for and enjoyed as much as possible by the children as well as by Esmeralda and Mario, the days of splendid summer were spent swimming and playing water games in the lake, the mornings for walks, on less warm days they went down the Trancura river and rainy days were a delight for everyone, because it meant going to the hot springs, what a wonderful feeling to enjoy semi-rustic thermal pools, built in the middle of the forest, with a stream on one side and the water that fed the pools on the other, their feet were massaged as they walked on the warm and ticklish pebbles, the inn with first class quality service and finesse. They were parallel years to the second life of hell and cavalry that Esmeralda lived with the father of her children, being a unique and magical life she enjoyed every summer, added to the pleasure trips to the Caribbean and the typical trip to the magical world of Disney, an opportunity in which they met and shared with a married couple, he being a gynaecologist and she a nurse from Santiago, Chile, and their only child, an eight-year-old boy, taking him also on the typical and dreamed trip of every child. The perfume that Esmeralda smelled was so exquisite, intoxicating and sublime that she approached the woman to delight herself with such an aromatic fragrance, and that was how when she was shopping for gifts and souvenirs, she looked for the perfume brand that became a part of her identity; she has been wearing it since 1996, that is, since the last century, a fragrance that identifies her and is unique and very attractive to the vast majority who smell it for the first time. "It is my natural scent", is the answer that she expresses with smiling confidence and pride to those who ask her, and despite the insistence she has never let anyone know the name of the perfume and even less the brand.

Regarding this there are two important episodes, one very emotional of her daughter Victoria, who was on a student exchange in Belmont, in the State of Colorado, United States. When she missed and suffered the absence of her mother, she would go to the mall with the pretext of looking for fragrances, but it was the imperative need to feel close to her mother through the perfume.

In relation to her perfume, there are several stories and anecdotes. William, one of her lovers, loved to approach and sit very close to her, to get intoxicated with her unique aroma. Once, he stopped at a well-known mall to buy her one, when they arrived at the store the saleswoman informed them that the product was out of stock, and offered them other brands explaining that they were similar and even more aromatic, but they said no, that the perfume they needed to buy was that precise one and not another, the saleswoman insisted that there weren't any left but that in the other store there were two units left; and told them that the perfume they wanted was discontinued.

–What? What does that mean, are they not going to make it anymore? Esmeralda asked in a terrifying and surprised voice. No, noooo, it can't be, that perfume is the essence of my being, it's the perfume that identifies me, it's a part of me, of my being, it's my identity and personality! And it was true, she wasn't exaggerating.

–In that case you should go to the other store and buy the last two units before they sell it to another client. Wait, let me check to see if it's in stock at another one of our stores she kindly added and with the clear intention of wanting to help.

–Yes please, William begged, with a tone of infinite gratitude and concern.

This is how they visited every store that the saleswoman indicated, each fragrance shop they came across on their way. They managed to buy more than thirty bottles of perfume, she should have been more than happy, never in her whole life had she bought, rather, had she been given so many bottles of perfume at one time and in one day. However, she was very sad and frustrated, and it wasn't something of a spoiled little girl, no, not at all, it distressed her too much to imagine herself without her perfume. What was she going to do when the last drop of fragrance from the last bottle ran out? Her anguish and concern was so much that she got to the point of starting to ration the amount she applied by using less, and stopped doing her romantic ritual every night of spraying the bedroom a couple of times over the bed to feel and intoxicate the atmosphere with her presence, causing an irresistible night of passion and lust. Yes, she loves making love, it is like her daily food and she prepares herself to truly enjoy it.

In the waking up to her new life as an independent woman, as a divorcee, she was experiencing the joy of feeling free, of being the owner of her time, there was no greater pleasure than having the freedom to do whatever she pleased, hangout with whoever she wanted without anyone criticizing her way of acting and being: "look at how you dress, you look like a whore", "you're not going anywhere, don't even think about it", "all those who call themselves your friends are such bad women, some are even tramps", etc., etc. Those phrases were a part of the past that appeared from time to time in her head, with the force of lightning on a rainy and stormy winter night, provoking memories of deep pain. However, the motivating force of her change, divorced and without the slightest interest in entering into a new relationship, with the dazzling personality of a strong, empowered woman, with a unique beauty and intelligence, surrounded herself with great friendships, especially men, of whom she enjoyed the company. Nonetheless, she had to recognize the emergence of a certain fragility with the appearance of feelings of friendships that could have easily turned into something more, something that she did not want and avoided at all costs; she was so happy with her life as a divorced, independent, and self-controlled woman, that it never crossed her mind to take a step back, to become a married, male-dominated woman again. She thought that everything beautiful that she had built in her friendships could disappear by becoming a couple and living a life of violence and heartbreak again, so no, no and no, a second marriage despite being better than the first was not at all in her plans, "case closed", as Dr. Polo would say. She made wonderful friends, one for each of her needs and interests, one for each day of the week, just like her purses and shoes, a special one that would match her and her clothes very well; she was surrounded by countless friends who were mostly men, apart from a couple of friend groups she had for tea and birthday celebrations, in addition to the group of colleagues and friends from work.

Yes, they were three wonderful groups of friends built over the years, experiencing feelings of happiness and empowerment with the new awakening to the life of a divorced, free and independent woman. Esmeralda also counted with the great friendship, love and unconditional support of her group of friends called *"Los Marynellos"*, who were the handkerchief for her tears, consolation, support and containment in the difficult moments of her life, such as cancer and unemployment, and the worst, when transforming into a real sea of tears for not being able to see and enjoy her endearing and adorable little grandchildren.

"Los Marynellos"

They were friends with whom she frequently met, and in particular for birthday celebrations, Valentine's Day, preparation of themed dinners, contests, national and costume parties, going out to bars and restaurants, in short, there was never a reason not to hangout. And the ritual walks on the beach, swimming to the buoys with the Pinto brothers was a delight: Raúl the conqueror, and Pato, still in his sixties, madly in love and crazy about his high school sweetheart; Fiorello, the group's artist, painter and writer; Eloísa, who little by little drifted apart from the group until they lost her, she cared a lot about her; Cristian, a lawyer and a close friend of Marcelita, she was super sweet, delicate, thoughtful and good at organizing reunions and celebrations; Marinela, the hostess, yes, her house had become the social headquarters; Sarita, a very sweet social worker colleague, like Cecilia; Marcia, on the other hand, was strong and a natural leader of the community, owner of the La Sala coffee shop, she was a great businesswoman, just like María Ester, with her beautiful boutique hotel La Casona; and Silvana, with her kindergarten Rayün Montessori, where Esmeralda's grandchildren attended, a friend who allowed her to visit and share with her little grandchildren, since she was not able to visit them whenever Victoria got angry and threw temper tantrums, as she used to punish her with whatever she felt was the most hurtful, forbidding her from enjoying the company and love of Viccencito and Doménica. Without a doubt, her network of friends and little angels, as she used to call them, were her pride and support.

Thursday nights were casino nights, technically drinks at the casino bar nights, because her friend, as a political authority, was forbidden to gamble, and she occasionally tried her luck by playing a few minutes on one of the slot machines. Her friend Alfredo, as usual, would pick her up at eight o'clock at night and return her home after midnight, a true Copiapó man, he knew the Atacameña traditions and its people, he was the leader of one of the right-wing parties, with great influences at local and national level, he lacked hours of the day to share interesting topics of conversation, such as regional development, new projects in his portfolio, the need for greater regional independence, being the centralization disastrous for the development of the regions, the approval of new mining projects, the issue of pollution, the scarcity of water resulting from mining overexploitation and the unlimited use of this precious and vital natural resource, obviously there was also a bit of gossip and comments regarding the actions of certain personalities, which the local press published, new couples, divorced couples, alarming them with part of the event, being generally the same, and the priority was to talk about the wellbeing of his beloved Atacama land. To all this, Esmeralda was the adoptive daughter of Atacama, she was born in the countryside, in Pichidegua, and after graduating from university at age 21, she came to Diego de Almagro identifying with the area to such an extent that every time she was asked about where she was from, she responded smiling and very proud:

–I'm from *Copiapó,* from the *III Región de Atacama*, in *Norte Chico,* Chile, not from San Pedro de Atacama as many tend to confuse, sending European tourists to Calama and not Copiapó, a fact that was very unfortunate and detrimental for the touristic development of the region.

And she would add in a tone of pride and sarcasm at the same time:

–How could anyone confuse our wonderful and beautiful region of Atacama, rich in natural tourism, surrounded by colourful hills, untamed dunes, highland lagoons, kilometres of beautiful beaches, being the driest desert in the world, where after a few hours of rain (an event which rarely occurs although in recent years it has been happening more frequently) serious natural disasters occur such as floods that have washed everything away from houses, cars and even public lighting, and the regrettable loss of human life, and the phenomenon of the flowery desert, a unique natural spectacle worldwide, where the arid hills covered with dusty sands and rocks are transformed into carpets of wild flowers, standing out from the roadside and seen from an aeroplane high in the sky, the fuchsia, yellow, white, and light blue colours.

During her first years of separation, still in the process of mourning and destroyed by the lack of communication with her children, she acquired the habit of going to the casino, to the point of becoming a gambler. She would wake up playing and drinking whisky, night became day, she would win and lose, she remembers spending all the money she had in cash, she'd continue with the credit cards waiting for midnight to pass so that the system would automatically allow another cash withdrawal. It was months and months of this behaviour, until one day she reacted when she woke up with her torso on the bed and her legs hanging down on the floor, still wearing her jacket, the bedroom and patio door wide open. It was shocking to hear the jeep's engine running, she didn't know how she got home, she imagines that she barely managed to get out of the jeep and fell asleep, exhausted, on the edge of the bed.

Thank God that in those years there was still not so much evil and the guardian angels continued to protect her. It would have been so easy for someone to steal the car, since the keys were still inside, the engine running and the electronic gate open. She will never get tired of giving infinite thanks to God for his immense love and great mercy. This was the incident that made her react and regain her sanity, she remembers that there were times in which she didn't even have money to eat because she had spent it all at the casino, feeding on what her neighbour Elsita would bring over, and her beloved and endearing friend, Carmelito Dinucci.

Carmelito who would invite her to eat a free snack at his restaurant or would personally prepare her a sandwich, she loved Carmelito as much or more than her own father, he was the handkerchief to her tears when she wasn't allowed to see her adorable little grandchildren or in moments of sickness or unemployment.

With her loved friend Carmelito and Vicchencito

The same thing happened to her little brother Jaime and even worse, because he lost both of his homes and was left with debt for several years, Esmeralda's older sister, the skinny one, continues to gamble, she always says that she does it as a distraction and because she always wins, which in practice isn't quite like that, it's common to see her go to her mother asking for money to cancel a debt or for fuel for her car, in the case of Esmeralda, her saint mother, "who always saves and always has", also got her out of trouble on more than one occasion, in urgent situations related to her health, and saved her from having her house auctioned off for non-payment. With her friend Jacky, they shared and were each other's support system, especially on Sundays, when they had lunch and cried their sorrows;

they bewailed and wondered why they had been so unlucky in their marriages, if they could have been blessed, form a nice family, since they had everything to be happy: beautiful, healthy and intelligent children, an excellent financial situation, and both had only dated once, marrying deeply in love with the thought that it would be for forever.

After the separation it was impossible to share as a family, due to the intolerance and incompatibility with her ex-husband; the couple of times they tried it was a real failure, since as always he would start making hurtful comments and jokes of bad taste, undermining and destructive, creating a tense and unpleasant environment for all, reason why they chose to have the children spend Christmas with both of them separately, alternating each year, a fact that only happened the first year, since he wouldn't allow them to share with Esmeralda when it was her turn, dragged by his dominance and oppressive, controlling and blackmailing love. Blaming her and playing the victim were common things he did and a part of his personality, with a unique facility to cry and shed tears. On the other hand, Esmeralda, who had suffered and cried during her almost twenty years of marriage and three of dating, had learned to control her emotions as a protection mechanism and for her psychological health, so much so that in moments of family crisis she emotionally protected herself by using her resilient mechanisms, to such an extent that she didn't shed a single tear, even if she wanted to, being alert to each blow and slap. In the silence and solitude of her home, she cried without consolation.

Remembering Christmas, the most important and transcendental date for a family with a Catholic tradition like hers, where the celebration of the end of the year holidays were around the birth of baby Jesus, she felt unappreciated and abandoned and tried to occupy her time by keeping herself busy. One Christmas she decided to dedicate it to HIV/AIDS patients benefiting from the Caritas Diocesana Copiapó food and emotional and spiritual support program; it was a personal initiative, and she turned to her friends who enjoyed the comfort of an excellent financial situation to give her food baskets to take to each of those patients, who were about fifteen. This is how she managed to gather a considerable amount of baskets, made up of what was necessary to prepare a Christmas dinner, and at six in the afternoon, when she'd finish work, she started the journey to each of the homes of her respected and beloved beneficiaries, with whom she maintained a relationship almost of friendship, because beyond being beneficiaries they had created a bond of friendship, trust and loyalty. The vast majority lived alone or with same-sex partners, in marginal and very poor areas, on the outskirts of town.

Those were visits of profound emotion and love, each one was pleasantly surprised by the visit of their social worker, whom they received with astonishment, but also with infinite joy and gratitude. Many invited her to come and even share what they had for dinner, or just offered her a glass of water. She made a stop on her way to participate in the midnight mass at a small chapel near the house she had just visited, and despite trying to go unnoticed and sit on the back benches to meditate, to take in the experience to find herself and herself with the heavenly Father, the chapel's catechists recognized her and let the priest know of her presence, actively incorporating her in the celebration of the Holy Eucharist with one of the readings from the Bible and helping the priest finish the last communion bread that had been left after the Eucharistic celebration, a ceremony of mostly anxious children awaiting the arrival of Santa Claus who, according to customs and traditions, would arrive after midnight to leave presents; it was ideal for them to participate in the mass so that the parents had the necessary time to drink the glass of *cola de mono* (a traditional Chilean Christmas drink, prepared with milk, coffee and brandy) and the slice of *pan de Pascua* (a traditional Chilean cake), or a glass of Coca-Cola and Christmas cookies that the children had prepared and cooked with a lot of love and effort to give to Santa, they also left carrots for the reindeers. At the end of the midnight mass, she visited three more homes in the midst of darkness, barking dogs and children who sounded happy and excited with their toys. It was an unforgettable Christmas, where tears of pain turned into tears of joy, emotion and brotherly love. The next morning, awake and happily tired, she reflected on what she had done, and a sense of panic and deep guilt came over her because she had used such humble people to appease her loneliness and lack of love and companionship from her children and grandchildren. She ran in search of her spiritual guide and asked to be urgently confessed because she had committed a very serious sin, she couldn't resist the guilt and pain; she needed to confess, receive a severe punishment and do the consequent penance. The priest welcomed her with infinite love and kindness, surprising her with his words.

–Dear child of God, you have not committed any sin and there's nothing to forgive. You are a very virtuous woman; who could have come up with doing such beautiful work of love on Christmas night, such as going to visit our brothers and sisters considered lepers, rejected by society? You have given them love, dignity and respect with your visit, they will value and appreciate it for life, and not only for satisfying their basic need for food, but for giving them love. Dear child of God, go home to rest and enjoy God's love.

With respect to the Christmases, she had to spend without her children, where crises of anguish and panic overwhelmed her, even leading to suicide attempts, when she reacted and sought out help in a state of crisis and emergency, one of her friends, a psychiatrist and psychologist she cared for and trusted, made her to react strongly:

–Stop playing happy family, that's been over for a long time now, do it for your well-being and for your children's.

She understood that the holidays, whether they are Christmas, birthdays or New Years, can be celebrated on any day, they didn't necessarily have to be celebrated on the exact day; this made a huge difference in her life and gave a meaning to it and she began to celebrate Christmas with her children on the same day but at lunchtime, making an exquisite Christmas meal and ending it with presents. She could do it a day early or a day after, it didn't make any difference, the important thing was to share and enjoy love in the company of her children. She reinvented herself and adapted to adversity so as not to succumb and die, she became a resilient person, which allowed her to transform herself into a happy and grateful woman, thankful for life and God, devoid of attachments and expectations, fully enjoying a starry night as well as a pitch dark one, a rainy day as much or more than a warm day, a sunrise and a sunset, in short, savouring each new day wherever she was.

The beginning of a new and overwhelming grand love

When she worked as executive director of a charitable foundation in northern Chile, she was invited to participate in an international convention on the aging of the population worldwide and the challenges that governments would have to face with the implementation of new social policies. It was a long and tiring night on a bus ride of over twelve hours. After arriving to Santiago, she had to hurry to reach the hotel in time to check in and take a much needed shower before embarking on the three-day training and analysis of public policies on aging.

When she arrived at the hotel, she was informed that the bus that would be taking the participants to the convention was about to leave, barely having time to literally throw her suitcase at the front desk and getting on the bus. She felt very uncomfortable for not wearing the appropriate clothes for the level and size of the event (which had to be formal attire and not leather pants and a sweater). In short, she took on as always, with the best possible disposition, the unforeseen event. Upon arriving at the CEPAL conference venue, the room was absolutely packed, with only a couple of seats available in the central circle; she found a seat and quickly began to speak with the person on her left, they reviewed the program of presentations and the participation of expert professionals from renowned world-class organizations. At that point, the event began and after the formal greetings the first exhibitor began speaking. Hearing his voice made her heart beat like crazy, as if it was going to burst out of her chest, it was a special and incredible sensation, as if she had known that person all her life. She felt extremely attracted and in shock, and as the man continued to talk the adrenaline flowed through her sweaty body; the exhibitor spoke in English and she didn't understand a single word, English was always a nightmare for her at school. Valery, the Bolivian representative, did the Spanish translation; they were seated about a couple of meters away and despite the short distance it was impossible for her to see them due to the wide circular shape of the narrow table, so as to call it something, until she couldn't control her curiosity, she leaned over her books and in that moment when she saw him, she froze, he was so, so handsome, and his voice resonated more in her heart than in her ears. It was a unique situation, as if they had known each other forever, from other past lives, she felt an attraction and an overwhelming love for him, she couldn't believe it and couldn't find an explanation for it. She dedicated herself to listening carefully to each sound he made as he spoke, not understanding a single word because she couldn't understand English at all. At last, his presentation ended and it was the second exhibitor's turn; during coffee break, and among the crowd of attendees and exhibitors she couldn't find him, she even thought it had been an hallucination. The break ended, and she was approached by her peers from other regions and professionals in the area, with whom she had a great affinity and interest in sharing experiences of the development of local work. Once the day was over, they went to lunch, and when coming back from the bathroom she saw him, yes, she saw him again, it wasn't a fantasy or a dream or hallucination, he was there, sitting on a black leather chair, he looked tired, or perhaps uncomfortable while hearing everyone speak in Spanish and he was unable to express himself other than in English. Valery was standing beside him talking with a couple of people, what happened then she didn't understand how, she really couldn't explain it, her attraction towards him was so powerful that it guided her steps directly to where he was sitting, and approaching Valery she said:

–Valery, please, please, can you introduce me to your friend –she asked in a pleading tone as she looked at him out of the corner of her eye and very nervous, her heart beating so fast that it felt like it was going to burst out of her chest.

–Esmeralda, how dare you? I can't, or don't you know who he is?

Very surprised and uncomfortable she replied:

–No, I don't know –and insisted again that she introduced her to her friend–: Please, Valery, introduce me –in a pleading tone she begged and begged, and suddenly he reacted when he noticed they were talking about him, he looked at Valery and with his hands facing up asked:

–What's going on? –or at least that's what she understood according to his body language.

Valery responded that Esmeralda was asking her to introduce him to her. He, smiling and flirtatious and shaking his hands in approval responded:

–Ok, introduce us.

–Alright, Todd, this is Esmeralda, she works for Caritas Copiapó.

And she exclaimed anxiously:

–Please, Valery, tell him that I wish to invite him for a walk to go sightseeing in Santiago, at this point Valery seemed increasingly more uncomfortable, although she managed to pass down the message.

Smiling he responded:

–No, thank you.

She, with her hands raised and shrugging her shoulders, made a gesture of resignation.

–I warned you, Esmeralda, that it was imprudent.

Esmeralda, with a stern voice and airs of pride, reacted with a defiant and sarcastic tone:

–Ah, tell him that a Chilean man would never say no to a woman, even less cordially inviting him out for a stroll.

To which he replied:

–If I'd had known, I would have said yes!

However, Esmeralda had stopped trying and had gone back to the conference room. Despite the great attraction she felt for him, she focused on the conference and began to share and personally get to know the colleagues with whom she used to communicate by phone and correspondence.

The next day, the conference room was once again packed. She saw a seat available at the other end of the famous and extensive table, she went there to find a seat, and as she passed between two rows of seats she saw him, he was looking at her with very smiling and mischievous eyes, but she grinned at him and continued walking until she sat down. They were in the middle of the first presentation, Esmeralda taking notes, when suddenly she felt someone touch her right shoulder, it was him, yes! It was him, he was squatting next to her, he spoke in English with obvious nervousness, she didn't understand anything, but he insisted on his mission, so much so that she finally understood that he was inviting her to get coffee:

–Sorry, I'm sorry, but no, I can't, I'm listening to the conference, later – he walked away and she could see him from where she was standing, he looked uncomfortable while she was out of place, she couldn't understand why she had rejected him, she felt very afraid, terrified.

A few minutes later he left the room, during break she looked for him and Valery acted as the interpreter, he asked about availability in the agenda to get together with Esmeralda, and she replied at each attempt:

–No, it's not possible, you can't, you have an interview scheduled with X –he would reply then by giving an alternative time, always receiving the same negative answer:

–No, you can't, you have an interview scheduled or a reunion with so and so at that time.

–At night then –he was saying now in almost a pleading tone, everything seemed so ridiculous and absurd seeing him beg when in fact he was the boss, not her. It was impossible to arrange a meeting no matter how hard they tried, he shrugged his shoulders and with a frustrated look he said goodbye.

Later he approached her during one of the breaks and told her that the next day they could get coffee together at the start of the event. Finally arranging a get-together, which she couldn't believe, Esmeralda approached the professional with whom she had sat down the first day; turns out that Jessica was from the North like her, had moved to the United States and lived in Manhattan working at an important organization for the elderly. She told her about the situation, asking her to please teach her to speak a little English so that she could communicate with him the next day. Jessica, very surprised, asked her:

–Esmeralda, do you know who he is?

–No, only that I like him a lot and that there's a strong energy or supernatural chemistry between us, I don't know what to call it, it's really powerful and it unites us from a lifetime, from our past lives, as if we know each other from past times, we love each other from those years.

Jessica, stunned by what she was hearing, tried to make Esmeralda react and warned her about who he was, she told her his name and position, but neither the name –Todd– nor the organization were familiar to her; her goal was to learn at that moment, already, the basics of English to be able to establish a conversation with him the next day.

They agreed to meet at the end of the working day. Typical: they started the express English class with greetings and introductions, Jessica would write in English for Esmeralda and she would do the same but in Spanish, and little by little she asked her to translate somewhat more daring and audacious questions and phrases, such as "you're very handsome", "I like you a lot" and others like that. Jessica, emphatically, replied:

–Esmeralda, how dare you, you can't say that.

–Fine, but at least write it down so I know how to say it…

Jessica finally caved in and wrote her a long list of phrases, from "hello" to wanting to know everything about him and expressing how attracted she felt, until the point of believing she was facing love at first sight, but with a past that went back to medieval times.

That night she barely slept, she woke up studying the phrases and thinking about what to wear to look stunning, although she didn't have much to choose from since she had only taken with her a pair of suits and trousers. That morning the conference began, and according to the plan with Todd, she didn't enter the room. she sat down waiting for him in the same armchair where she had boldly approached him the day before. About fifteen minutes passed and he still hadn't arrived, until she saw him walking at a steady pace, with a briefcase in one hand and the other in his trouser pocket under his long dark brown raincoat, very formal and elegant, in a grey suit, white button up shirt, and green tie with a gold and brown design. He walked in a long stride and looked extraordinarily interesting and manly next to the famous Valery, with whom he was conversing at the same time. Valery was very surprised to see that he approached to greet Esmeralda, who responded with a kiss on the cheek.

Todd said goodbye to Valery and showed Esmeralda the stairway that led to the cafeteria located on the second floor. With a beautiful and wide smile, she answered:

–Let's go –and he looked at her pleasantly surprised. *(Let's go)*

Yes, so far Jessica's expressed English class was having the expected effects and even exceeding them; he ordered two coffees, asking ~~if~~ her if she wanted milk and sugar with it, to which she replied radiantly:

–No, thank you, just plain coffee, please.

–Wow! You speak English?

She looked at him smiling mischievously as she carried her coffee towards one of the cafeteria tables, absolutely empty at that moment. They were invaded by a sense of complicity, joy and nervous excitement; they looked and acted like a pair of teenagers. He would say to her:

–I love your smile, it is very cute –and she, reading her English notes, responded:

–You are very handsome.

Both, nervous and blushing, continued with their interrogation, intrigued to know a little more about each other; everything was valid to communicate, they used hand gestures, grinned and made faces, body language, etc, etc, counting children with their hands, "yes, three", "me too, two girls and one boy", "no, really, I also have three kids".

–Wow, me too.

There couldn't be more coincidences.

–I'm a manager.

–Me too.

Todd pointed to her ring finger asking if she was married, and she responded with gestures and shaking her hands and head from side to side in denial:

–No, no, I'm separated.

He, pointing to his chest with his index finger, added:

–Me too.

–How long?

–Two years.

–Me too.

And that's how with gestures and faces like a mime, more than two hours passed by, they were absolutely enchanted with each other's company; it was evident that they both felt a great attraction. Already more confident and entering the conversation, Esmeralda began to loosen up and read some of the more specific questions about work, deliberately skipping the most daring phrases, and since she didn't know how to pronounce well, he asked her to see what was written on the sheet of paper, until carelessly he snatched it from her and read each of the questions and comments. He was very happy and pleasantly flattered; he had read everything she hadn't been able to because of modesty and nervousness. During that, Valery appeared looking like a bossy old woman, and with a firm voice said:

–Todd, Todd, it's time for your next meeting.

They didn't want to say goodbye, he said "let's have lunch together", but she replied in a bothered tone:

–No, impossible.

They said goodbye, continuing on with their working day, she was on cloud nine and with a smile from ear to ear, while Jessica waited for her with overflowing curiosity. She told her that everything had been fabulous and thanked her for her vital support.

After all this, it was already the end of the third and last day of conferences. After the break, and sitting in the room with her friend

Jessica (yes, at that point they were already great friends), he came over and sat next to her, talked to Jessica and she told him that he should give the closing speech at the event. Right there and then, Esmeralda realized that he wasn't just another professional who attended the congress, he was a great authority worldwide, but wasn't sure whom he represented.

Unfortunately, she had a doctor's appointment with her doctor of almost two years, as a result of her severe depression, which she couldn't miss; she explained to Jessica that she had to leave and to please tell Todd to walk her out to say goodbye. He chivalrously answered her and told her that he was sorry, that he couldn't leave because he had to give the speech, but Esmeralda insisted that it would only be a couple of minutes. So, he got up and accompanied her. They walked in silence through two long corridors and crossed a large hall until they reached the main exit of the venue, from where she could grab a taxi to get to her therapy appointment. They looked at each other with elusive nervousness and suddenly he gave her a strong and wonderful hug while deeply sighing; she completely let herself go to the embrace, and without saying another word they said goodbye. She watched him disappear as he walked quickly back to the room.

Upon arriving at the doctor's appointment, he obviously saw that something new was happening with his patient, it was evident, she looked extremely happy, her eyes shone like two stars and she wouldn't stop smiling and even sighing like a fifteen-year-old totally in love. The doctor was very pleased to see her so happy, however, he made her see that it could have just been a meeting between two people in a conference and only that, and that since she was very emotionally weak and lacking love, she could have seen and felt more than what it actually was. He asked her to be prudent and cautious, not to be surprised if she didn't receive any kind of communication from the person she had just met and with whom she thought she was in love. But it was impossible to bring her down from cloud nine and from the state of euphoria in which her heart and even her soul were in, she insisted that they knew each other from past lives and that it was their destiny to meet again, that they both loved each other and that now was the moment to make that grand love a reality that had been forbidden in the past.

The person who returned to Copiapó was definitely not the same person, it was a different woman, absolutely happy and in love who day dreamed. She remembers that the next day she went to the beach to enjoy the day and during the whole trip while she was driving with the windows down, she was listening and singing to a CD of the greatest romantic hits of the 80s, with her long and silky black hair flying with the wind, she would look up, and as she saw a plane pass, she felt that it was Todd crossing in the transparent sky.

On Monday, returning to work, Lucita, her devoted and beautiful secretary, was also surprised to see her boss so radiant and happy, and asked her:

–Ms. Esmeralda, it's noticeable that everything went well in Santiago, I'm really happy for you.

At noon the bishop's secretary called her saying that she had received an email in English addressed to her. Wow, he had written her! She knew Todd would write to her even though her doctor had tried to prepare her for the opposite. The bishop's secretary stated:

–Alright, I took the liberty of replying, since it was a very short email greeting you and asking if you had arrived safely home; it also said that he was thinking about you. It was signed with the name Todd.

–Oh, that's amazing, thank you so much!

–I replied yes, that you had arrived safely and that you appreciated his concern and greeting.

That email was the beginning of their romantic relationship and overwhelming passion that would lead her to re-awake love and sexuality in the broad sense of the word and an openness to the world, with dream trips wherever he had a meeting or conference of international nature.

The first trip was to São Paulo, Brazil then it was Brussels, Belgium, Washington DC, United Sates, and countless other countries. They enjoyed their loving and passionate encounters like a teenage couple, although the distance shattered their existence. However, the love that united them was so great that they could withstand physical distance and it made them take advantage of every available second, they had in those fleeting and fiery three days (or at most a week), once a month or every two, and that's how almost three years passed of burning love and passion.

Ipanema beach Brazil

CHAPTER II

Six months in London, once in a lifetime experience

Esmeralda, with the rebirth of her life, decided to make a drastic change, and took the bold decision to go to London, England to study English, leaving everything behind, her family, friends, loved ones and her Atacama land.

The idea of studying English wasn't hers, but instead was from her beloved friend Ricardo, an intellectual man, lawyer, voracious reader, sybarite, with a fine taste for good wine. They were united by their love for public service and the pleasure of drinking an exquisite Scottish whisky, during entertaining and interesting topics of conversations, debating current events, national and international activities related to economic, political and social development, and always concerned about the well-being of the community. As good friends; and as expected, they shared personal matters; that is how a few days after Esmeralda's car accident, she called him to meet up, because she needed to talk with her friend, tell him that she wasn't in a good place and that she needed to do something with her life.

After telling him the details of the car accident, ordering a couple of good Scottish whiskies to drive the pain and fright away and catching up, Esmeralda commented frustrated and tired:

–You know, something is going on with me, I don't feel good; in fact, I'm not in a good place.

Ricardo exclaimed as he shrugged his shoulders:

–But it's obvious, you almost died, any person in your position and right mind would feel the same or worse, right?

–Yes, I know I dodged a bullet, the accident could have been worse, I could have even died and I wouldn't be here with you now –she replied apologetic and grinning.

–You see, everything is fine, stop crying and let's order another round of whisky – looking at the bartender he raised his hand saying–: two more whiskies, please.

–No ice, please – Esmeralda added.

They continued talking, but Esmeralda seemed uneasy and uncomfortable, so he asked her:

–Ok, let's see, what's wrong, is there something else that you haven't told me? Because you don't seem fine, something's wrong. he commented, while frowning and scratching his head.

–You finally understand me and notice it, see? I no longer even feel like going to the office, and you know how much I like to do social projects and work, but not locked up and spending all day sitting in front of a computer, I miss being in contact with people, apart from the fact that the atmosphere in the office you could say isn't the best, there are a couple of harpies who were even happy with my accident.

–But how, how is that possible?

–What, you don't believe me? They are more bitter than a potato tree.

Ricardo innocently laughed.

–It's obvious that people like that exist everywhere, amen to the fact that you don't have to please the whole world. Well, there are exceptional cases such as myself –he chuckled.

–Yes, of course, you have it –she added ironically and changing her voice said–: Ricardo, it's getting late.

–And, what's the rush?

– "Solitude" and "Hope"

–Stop being so melodramatic, mmm, what do you think about doing an English course?

–What, are you crazy? Are you laughing at me? You know how bad I am with languages.

–I'm being serious –Ricardo replied.

–Just stop, impossible, I can't even say hello in English.

–Stop exaggerating, let's see, how do you say hello in English?

–Hello! Obviously, everyone knows how to say hello in English.

–Remarkable! You said it perfectly; you can even pass as a Yankee, hahaha! No, stop joking, I'm being serious.

–Yeah, stop fooling around and pulling my leg, that idea is more than crazy, English is too hard for me, you know that I even change the station on the radio to not listen to a song if I have no idea what they are singing, I've always been afraid of making a fool out of myself by humming a song that I have no clue what they're saying and me happily singing, perhaps they're talking about the devil, or killing Clinton or the Pope, you know how crazy some people are.

–You know we're talking pure nonsense, think about it and then we'll talk.

–The next day, Esmeralda woke up thinking that perhaps the idea of studying English wasn't too crazy, apart from the fact that she needed it in order to communicate with Todd. The truth is that it's becoming more and more necessary to speak English and it is a plus for jobs, and for travelling, and she liked that so much.

That's how she spent the whole week mulling over the subject until finally she made up her mind and went to Santiago to find and buy a six month English course; six months seemed like a sensible period of time, because in a month she wouldn't be able to learn anything, in three months she would just be getting the hang of it, and six months was an ideal time to study and it was prudent for her to ask for a leave of absence from the office.

She began the preparations to undertake her crazy trip to the British capital with joy and an exquisite adrenaline rush, with the support and company of her daughter Renata, who was studying at the university, like her son Apollo; they both lived in Santiago and shared an apartment. Renata thought her mother's idea was a good one, and after visiting several travel agencies, she decided on one that offered her a complete study package, which included everything from tickets to the school pass, besides the six month English course, student visa and homestay with a British family.

As soon as she returned to Copiapó, Esmeralda, first thing Monday morning, spoke with her boss, letting her know the decision she had made, and explaining that she needed a six-month leave of absence without pay, to which she responded astonished:

–What? It can't be, you can't leave like this! I just took office and you're my trusted professional, I need you.

–I know, I'm truly sorry, but I've made the decision, look, I have the vouchers here with the payment of the course and tickets.

–Wow, you've rushed this! You should have sent the permission request to the minister first.

–I know, but I couldn't wait, I already made the decision, I'm so sorry for you, Teresa, but I need to make a pause in my life, I'm really exhausted and stressed, and a very complex time is coming due to the presidential elections, and to be honest, I don't wish to be involved in political campaigns nor anything related to that matter.

–Alright, well in that case if you've already made the decision and have already bought the tickets, there's nothing else to do. I will send your letter to the minister Laura.

–Thank you very much.

That same afternoon she received a call from the minister. Laura was very upset and almost yelling, she spoke nonstop on the other end of the line:

–Esmeralda, how did it cross your mind that you could leave for six months? Impossible! You can't just leave your job, you're a trusted professional to the president of the republic, and moreover we are in the middle of a leadership change in your region and, a lot of work is coming with the presidential elections for the re-election of our president Bachelet. No, you don't have permission!

–But, minister, I've already even bought the tickets –she added.

–I'm sorry, you should have asked me before making the decision –and she hung up the phone.

Esmeralda was left with the words in her mouth, without even having a second to insist, she was stunned, dumbfounded, she didn't know what to do. Trembling, she walked towards her boss's office to tell her and vent her feelings, and she responded with a slight degree of sorrow and understanding:

–It was to be expected that the minister would answer that way, you can't just suddenly leave one day, you're the assistant manager, trusted professional, and I truly need you.

–Yes, I know and I admit that I acted hastily, but I really don't want to be here anymore, I feel stressed and I wouldn't be able to help run a political campaign, it's not correct, I can't.

–Ok, well in that case you should quit, you have no other option –she responded shrugging her shoulders.

–Quit? Quit my position? And what will I do when I return from England? No, I'm sorry, I cannot quit –she said apologetic and sad.

–I see no other solution –Teresa intervened in a serious tone–: I'm sorry, there's nothing I can do to help you.

–I will write to the minister explaining my situation, I will insist on my request of leave –Esmeralda insisted in a decisive tone.

–Good luck –Teresa said goodbye in a soft tone as she resumed reading the documents she had on her desk.

Esmeralda returned to her office to continue working, walking at a slow pace, head down, very concerned and overwhelmed.

In an unusual way, she received an immediate response to her letter on behalf of the minister: the answer was negative, just as everyone expected except for her, to whom "no" didn't exist. In the face of the situation, her boss suggested that she wrote two letters and left them signed before travelling to London, a letter of leave without pay and the other presenting her resignation, the second letter being a strategy as a last alternative, in case the minister didn't change her mind.

Esmeralda distrusted the voluntary resignation letter, but understood that it was absolutely necessary if she finally didn't authorize her request of leave; otherwise, she would be sanctioned for abandoning her job and would be unable to return to a position in public service for five years; she was between a rock and a hard place, she had no choice but to accept Teresa's suggestion. That's how she did it and that's how they responded to her, as soon as she arrived in London, she received an email informing her that they had accepted her voluntary resignation. This position she held was very coveted, strategic and highly paid, and it was to be expected that other employees went after it. Ironically, it was taken by one of the harpies.

Those were days of great tension for Esmeralda in all aspects, starting with the workplace; she had to work harder than usual to hand over the position to her newly arrived boss, whose profession was a medical technologist, who didn't know the service and even less the complexity of public gender policies, how difficult it was to sensitize the other entities in the public sphere to comply with the demands of the central level, to incorporate the gender variable in the execution of public policies, talk about transvestism, gender gaps, inequality, indicators of impact and self-management, uff! That consumed days and days of her precious time, while having to focus as much as she could to finish up work and close programmes and projects as far as possible.

Another great issue was to vacate and rent her house, it was not easy or a matter of days, especially keeping in mind that in Chile it is customary to rent empty, unfurnished houses, unlike in other countries; another concern was her car and her adorable pet Sapphire, but all this became less important amidst the new and great event that awaited her and that she had to face, a fact of such importance that this would make her hesitate and rethink her project of travelling to London.

She had an unexpected family situation, and despite being really wonderful news, it made her hesitate about going on her study trip. Her role as a mother came first, even though the relationship with her children wasn't the best and the thought of staying, although it is true that it would contribute to supporting Victoria, wasn't always going to be possible due to the incompatibility with her ex-husband, who made it difficult for her and prevented her from having contact with them, manipulating them in an astute and successful way. It was his favourite strategy to harm and get revenge on Esmeralda for having left him.

The news in question was that she would be a grandmother, wonderful news without a doubt, but for her it was not the right moment. She was immersed in a nebula of contradictory feelings, on the one of hand, an infinite emotion and joy of just imagining herself being a grandmother, and knowing how much she liked children she was sure to be a very awesome grandmother and adored by her little grandchildren, and on the other hand, she was very nervous and under a lot of stress, she couldn't sleep, she was too anguished just thinking that if she travelled and something happened to her daughter during her pregnancy, she would never forgive herself, never in her life.

It was terrible, Esmeralda felt bad, feelings of guilt invaded her reinforced by her ex-husband's lapidary comments and judgments, who accused her of being a selfish and non-nurturing mother who only thought about her personal well-being and not that of her children, that it was inconceivable that she was thinking of abandoning her pregnant daughter, and even more because of Victoria's uncertain personal situation, with an incipient relationship and a university degree halfway done. It was impossible not to feel like the villain in the movie and she was hesitant to carry out her project of studying English abroad; she gathered the courage to visit those who would be her in-laws, the parents of her daughter's boyfriend whom she personally didn't know. She did know Vittorio's mother a little, as she had worked in the same public health service a few years ago; even so, she was encouraged thinking that they could be her card of salvation, because if her daughter had their support as future grandparents, they could help alleviate her great sorrow by supporting her during her absence. When she got to their house, Ximena, Vittorio's mother, opened the door, she was wearing a kitchen apron, sleeves rolled up and her hands were wet, she looked a bit surprised by Esmeralda's visit, but with a smile she invited her in:

–Hello, come in, come in, follow me to the kitchen, I'm making lunch –she made her come in and showed her the way through the narrow corridor up to the kitchen, where the warm daylight came in, announcing the prompt arrival of spring through a door that led to the patio and was slightly opened, the inside of the house smelled like freshly cooked food; Esmeralda's keen sense of smell and cat allergy alerted her of the presence of kittens, the pestilent odour, that she could perceive from miles away, caused her to sneeze.

–It was an atmosphere of coldness and nervousness, with a mixture of spice smells caused by the exquisite aroma of homemade food that came from the kitchen where Ximena was working hard preparing lunch. Esmeralda was making a great effort to converse and talk about the reason she was there, although it was more than obvious or perhaps not, as she later realized, that they had a different way of thinking and their concepts about life were literally opposite. Ximena was still busy cooking, with evident signs of nervousness as well as Esmeralda, who was trying to justify and explain her sudden visit. She had thought about starting the conversation by congratulating them because they were going to be grandparents just like her, and for the first time, it was a great blessing and family joy, and that the real and crucial objective of her visit was to ask them for all the possible support they could give to her beloved daughter during her absence. However, nothing was going according to the plan, even though the welcome from Ximena wasn't too bad, they spent about fifteen minutes in the kitchen talking about trivialities and avoiding the topic of interest, waiting for her husband to come down and join the family; her husband apparently was resting in their bedroom, on the second floor of the old and cosy family home. Between the handling of pots and utensils that she used for the variety of dishes that she was preparing simultaneously, at least five, such an appetizing smell came out that it was inevitable to make her mouth water, to the point that she had the audacity to put her nose in one of the pots and try a smoky stew of meat and seafood.

Meanwhile, Ximena commented that today's young adults were so much different than her youth years not to even think of her parent's time and even less of her grandparent's time, her future in-law said:

–Nowadays, young people's priorities are their studies, achieving a professional career, enjoying life, and they don't want anything to do with being in a serious relationship, they just want to enjoy and have a good time –without a doubt she was setting the stage by making Esmeralda feel that she couldn't count on their son, who wouldn't assume his role as a father, reinforcing and making it very clear with her following comments as a monologue:

–In fact, and without going any further, while I was in university, I got pregnant and had to get an abortion, because my priority was to finish my studies, I wasn't going to have a baby at that stage of my life; I was barely twenty years old.

"That explains a lot", Esmeralda said to herself with profound sadness and deception. She was scandalized by Ximena's comments, because Esmeralda was a strong Catholic woman, a fighter for life from the first second of conception, she would never agree to even touch on the subject of a possible abortion in her family, and even less in the case of the sacred life of her daughter and her grandson. At that moment Vittorio's father appeared, an aged and scruffy-looking man, who shook her hand to greet her and invited her to sit on an old armchair that smelled of cat pee and covered with hair, which caused an instant allergic reaction; in just a few seconds her beautiful dress was covered with cat hair, causing her great discomfort and an uncontrollably sneeze impossible to avoid. The aromatic freshness that came from the colourful flowers that decorated the coffee table, were her salvation to hold her breath, while trying to manage to start a conversation, the same they had in the smoky kitchen was repeated in the living room, but on this occasion also with the participation of the house owner, Vittorio's father; when Esmeralda realized that there would be no acceptance or reciprocity from them in the immense joy she felt knowing that she would become a grandmother, she realized that she wouldn't achieve her mission and said goodbye with a tone of plea, shame and sadness:

–I'm so grateful for your time and for welcoming me into your home as the mother of your son's girlfriend, I only ask you and would truly appreciate from the bottom of my heart, that my daughter Victoria could count with your support, and particularly with yours, Ximena, as a woman, mother and health professional, in the event that my daughter requires help if an emergency were to present itself during my absence.

–Don't worry, go on your trip, your daughter will be fine, nothing is going to happen to her, Ximena replied, showing relief that the uncomfortable meeting was over. On the other hand, Vittorio's father was more concise, limiting himself to saying:

–See you later, have a nice time, enjoy your trip.

They didn't say anything with regard to becoming grandparents.

Esmeralda left very sad when she realized that her daughter wouldn't be able to count on the support of her baby's father's family, for her it was very difficult to understand and accept, although knowing it made her look for other strategies and support groups: her midwife friends would undoubtedly support her, as they were united by a great friendship built over years of public service and personal and family growth.

Victoria's pregnancy brought to mind memories of her difficult pregnancy and the terrible circumstances in which she gave birth to her son Apollo, that event kept running through her mind and she prayed to God that her daughter's pregnancy and delivery would be of absolute normality and not like hers, so traumatic.

Her son Apollo was born on a cold, rainy and agitated winter night in Concepción, Chile, the medical staff made up mostly of medical and obstetrics intern students invaded the large and old maternity room of the Guillermo Grant Benavente Regional Hospital of Concepción, from where the young woman's heart breaking screams came, shocked and terrified by the painful symptoms of her first-born premature birth. What mostly scared and caused Esmeralda's screams, wasn't the physical pain but the risk of her son's death, who was not yet ready to be born, because he was barely six months pregnant. She would have given everything and more to prevent childbirth, delaying it until her child reached maturity and the nine months of gestation, but it was impossible because she had already entered the active phase of labour. Her screams and moans echoed through the lurid corridors of the old and cracked building that had withstood a few earthquakes and countless strong tremors, typical of a seismic country like Chile; her screams could be heard from far away without the copious and windy rain that hit the windows silencing them, making that night even more tenebrous. It was incredible to feel how that baby, with only twenty-eight weeks of gestation, would kick its mother's womb with an indomitable fierceness, as if it felt trapped and suffocated and was crying out to be born. The contractions, sharp and fast, did not wait, and after monitoring the intensity and frequency, the medical eminence of the moment raised his voice and ordered:

–Quickly take the patient to the delivery room, it's time, we can no longer wait –while at a steady pace they left the nurses' station.

–What's wrong? What's going on Johnny? –The young mother asked–: René, please answer me, what's happening? –Esmeralda shouted helplessly, adding–: Johnny, I can't give birth; I'm barely twenty-eight weeks pregnant.

Esmeralda begged, invaded by a terrifying fear as she looked with heart breaking eyes at her husband Mario, who tightly held her hands and snuggled his head next to hers, trying to calm her down while also trying to show strength to contain her and himself, but he too, was stunned and as concerned as she was. Johnny and René, her medical student friends, explained to them that the first phase of labour had already begun with an eight centimetre dilation, making it impossible to reverse the process and the delivery had to be completed as soon as possible to avoid other complication and/or infection to the baby.

–That's why, Esmeralda, when I asked your permission to perform a vaginal examination, it was to evaluate and find out what situation you were in, and I was able to clearly diagnose that you had started the active phase of labour due to the cervix dilation and your baby in birthing position, –Johnny explained.

–What? Johnny, are you telling me that my son is ready to come out? He's going to be born now, right now? –Esmeralda asked almost screaming, her face disfigured from the shock and concern. She dreamt of her first-born's arrival, but this wasn't the time, his premature birth could put his life at risk, and they weren't ready to receive him yet, they didn't even have diapers, not to mention a crib to lay him in. She knew that wasn't essential given the magnitude of what they were going through, but it was concerning for the young couple considering their life as university students without financial resources, who barely had enough to feed themselves. Esmeralda had not eaten properly during her pregnancy, there were even days where she went blank due to lack of food.

She remembered with sadness and very ashamed one day when she went to her university teacher's house to look for a book, the teacher kindly let her in and offered her coffee, and she, on the verge of fainting from the lack of food and in a state of obvious malnutrition, with a very sweet voice broken by shame, asked:

–Miss Ximena, thank you very much, you are so kind, but would it be possible to have some fruit, please?

–Yes, of course, what do you prefer, an orange or an apple?

Esmeralda, with the hunger she had, would have wanted both fruits, but considering her good manners with which she had been brought up, she opted for the bright and reddish apple that Miss Ximena showed her from the kitchen door.

–The apple, please –Esmeralda responded. That was the most exquisite, crunchy and juiciest apple that she remembers having eaten in her entire life.

Returning to the present, to the conversation with her intern friends:

–Yes, your baby is ready to be born, his head is even facing down, which is great because it'll be a normal and fast delivery – Johnny explained smiling, and proceeded in a more serious and accommodating tone–: that's why immediately after examining you I had them get the doctor on call to inform him of the beginning of your labour. But don't worry, everything will be fine, we will be with you during the delivery and until your baby is born. Stay calm, everything will be ok.

In the delivery room everything went quickly as Johnny had anticipated, although without the expected normality. René accompanied and emotionally supported Esmeralda due to the impossibility of Mario entering the delivery room, in those years the partner of the woman in labour was not allowed to be a companion in health centres, even less in public hospitals, but thank God she had the company and the unconditional support from her great university friends, who were able to access practically all the specialties of the hospital, as was the case of Johnny and René, senior medical students, and a couple of midwives and nurses, who were doing all their practices and internships and the last stage of their studies before acquiring their bachelor's degree. Fortunately, she counted with this wonderful support group that was crucial in the face of the unexpected and serious events that would occur during childbirth that rainy winter night, where there wasn't any medicine to counteract the pain, and the contractions became more and more intense, painful and followed one after another when stimulated with physiological saline in order to accelerate the last phase of labour; since the dilation of the cervix was sufficient to give birth, at that point it was impossible to reverse the premature process of labour, not even considering that there were still three months until the baby was full term.

–Push, push...! Esmi, push harder, Esmi, with all your strengths, it's time, your baby is about to be born! –René said while squeezing one of her hands and with the other in a fist gesturing "strength, strength" ... –Come on, you can do it!

–Aaaayyyy, aaayyy…! It's so painful, I can't take it anymore – Esmeralda shouted and moaned–: It hurts, it hurts so much! –she cried as she held on with one hand to the side bars of the bed and with the other tightly squeezing René's hand.

–He's coming...he's coming...we can see his head, push, push...give the last push with all your strength so your baby can come out – said the midwife who supported the gynaecologist.

–Scalpel, please, we need to make a couple more incisions – said the gynaecologist.

– Noooo, noooo, please! –Esmeralda screamed as though someone was killing her.

– He's coming out...he's coming out... –the midwife said with a loud voice.

– Ooohhhh, no! –the doctor suddenly almost yelled, very surprised.

– It's terrible! –the midwife also yelled.

– No, no…! It can't be, we need to get her to the operating room! –the gynaecologist replied.

Everyone runs out of the delivery room with the baby, even René. In that moment someone says:

–It seems that they are two, yes, another baby, help me, please, we need to continue assisting the patient.

–What's happening? What's going on? –Esmeralda shouted demanding an answer–: Where are they taking my baby? I want to see him, you can't take him, he's my baby, please, please! –she begged with heart breaking screams, wanting to get up from the bed with the fierceness of a mother whose newly born has been taken from her.

She suddenly felt herself fainting while at the same time receiving in her right arm a strong and sharp prick from a thick and cold needle. They chose to sedate her to calm her down and continue the delivery.

After a few hours, Esmeralda woke up in the postpartum recovery room, very sore, confused, dizzy and thirsty, with her lips dry and her tongue hanging out like a rag. She made an effort to catch one of the nurse's attention, who kindly approached her bed asking:

–How do you feel?

Esmeralda just exclaimed in a somnolent voice:

–Where's my baby? I want to see him, why did they take him away without letting me see him?

And she burst into tears, absolutely distraught. The nurse caressed her face and with a very sweet voice tried to calm and comfort her, and at the same time answered her questions:

–Don't worry, your baby is fine, we had to take him to the incubator because he's so small and his little lungs haven't yet fully developed, he still can't breathe on his own

–Ah! I had a baby boy? –Esmeralda asked–: Please...please... bring me my son, I want to see him and nurse him, look, milk is coming out of me, I have so much –she said smiling, showing how wet her hospital shirt was.

–An that precise moment, Mario and Johnny, strode into the room as if they were in a hurry and approached her bed, their faces clearly showing weariness and concern.

–Yes, yes, my dear Esmi, you had a baby boy –Mario murmured with a soft voice, showing a tender smile as he hugged her. They clung emotionally and tearfully to each other.

Esmeralda begged him to take her to her baby boy.

–Yes, yes, of course, my love, of course you can see and take care of our little boy.

Johnny, Mario and the nurse looked at each other trying to explain and give her the painful and hopeless news.

Mario cleared his throat to remove the lump that was tightening his throat, and began to speak:

–My love, my beloved Esmi, yes, we had a beautiful baby boy –tears streamed down his cheeks as he attempted to continue–: Our baby boy was born ill.

Esmeralda, very anxious and sobbing asked him, as she grabbed him by the sweater and shook him with her hands demanding that he tell her the truth:

–But, what's wrong with him, why do you say he was born ill?

–It's just that he is so small, they have him in an incubator, he's fighting for his life, we'll get through this together, I have plenty of faith that we will.

Esmeralda replied raising her voice, with confidence and certainty:

–Yes, yes, of course our son will recover and come out of this; I will nurse him, yes, with my breast milk he will gain weight and grow super fast, please bring him to me so I can start nursing him –she demanded looking at the nursing staff near them.

Mario couldn't answer; he wasn't able to tell her that her little boy had been born with a genetic malformation and that the chances of his survival were almost none, he couldn't believe it himself and even less, break Esmi's heart with such painful news. He was heartbroken, holding back a sea of tears that he tried to hold back. With a lump in his throat, and making a superhuman effort to maintain his strength and not burst into tears, he looked at Johnny pleading with his eyes and hinting that it was time to tell Esmeralda the truth. Johnny approached her and in a very soft voice began to tell her about her baby's health:

–Esmi, yes, we had to put your baby in an incubator to provide artificial ventilation, because as he is very small, his little lungs are not fully developed yet and he needs time to breathe on his own –Johnny explained with a fatherly air.

–That is why and with more reason, I need to nurse him so that he grows and recovers faster. Yes, please, Johnny, bring him to me, I want to see him and cuddle him, –Esmeralda said in a pleading tone. Then Mario broke down sobbing and caressing her like a little girl and said:

–My love, my beloved Esmi, the truth of the matter is that our little boy was born with a problem in his belly and they are going to operate on him today.

–What? It can't be! –she was left in a state of shock, but demanded they to tell her what was going on with her baby, she needed to know more.

–Don't worry, Esmi, our friends are supporting us, they've been super great, at seven o'clock, they contacted an eminent childrens' surgeon, Dr. Sergio Rojas, and he is going to perform an operation at 9 am today.

–Yes, in a little bit –Johnny said as he looked at his watch and nodded his head.

–But, what does my baby have? Why are they going to operate on him? What are they going to operate on? Ah! Is that why they ran out with him yesterday as soon as he was born? Please, tell me what's going on! I want to see him before they take him to the other hospital, please…please…! –she begged with an expression of infinite pain, a mother whose newly born had been taken from her for a second time, and without even giving her a chance to see him and hug him against her chest.

–Yes, of course you can see your baby before they transfer him –Johnny accepted.

Then he looked at his watch again and exclaimed:

–Oh, no! It's time –and ran out of the room catching up in a moment with the staff, in a second, the staff who had begun to transfer the baby through the cold and clean neonatology corridors, stopping them, and returned to where Esmeralda was, at the company of a nurse who was gently and firmly pushing the incubator. Inside was a miniature baby connected everywhere to an infinite number of cables and tubes, on his chest, arms, legs, nose and mouth, and his little heart beating at a thousand per hour, moving his tiny body in a surprising way, it seemed that he was going to explode and disintegrate. The nurse brought the incubator closer to Esmeralda's bed saying:

–Look, here's your little boy fighting for his life.

Esmeralda burst into tears while strongly sliding her hands over the incubator trying to touch, take, and caress her baby boy, she desperately needed to hug him, kiss him, protect him, and cradle him close to her chest. That wish couldn't be fulfilled due to the circumstances in which he was born and his critical state of health. They had to run, time was the essence, the ambulance was waiting and the ward was ready for its first surgery, and that was how Esmeralda saw her son for the first time, it was only a few seconds of contact between mother and son before he was taken and snatched away for the second time. It was a crucial and sufficient time that allowed her to convey her infinite and inexhaustible motherly love, energy, courage, strength and faith in God and in medical science to fight for his life. Faced with so much pain and anguish that oppressed her heart, she prayed and prayed with immense devotion and faith to God for her little boy's life, as she watched him leave in the incubator pushed by the nurse, followed and accompanied by Mario and Johnny. At that precise moment it occurred to her to call her son Apollo, a Greek name that means "the one who wards off death". Apollo is the god of the arts, of the day and the sun, son of Zeus and Leto. Later she would tell her husband of her decision.

–Our son will be named Apollo –she told him with joy, firmness and security–: Apollo is a name that radiates strength and a warrior's invincible power and wards off death.

Calling her son Apollo broke the great tradition sustained for decades in her husband's family of perpetuating in the first-born son the name of his father, grandfather, great-grandfather and great-great-grandfather, Mario Salvador, who could not refute the decision despite his strong character, misogyny and dominant personality, they were facing an exceptional situation, it was the life of his son, and bearing in mind Esmeralda's condition as a mother, who had made the decision as a strategy to protect and save her son's life, there was nothing to do, just abide by it and pray for the life and health of his son, now beginning to call him by his name Apollo.

That was the traumatic way in which Esmeralda, the pilgrim bride, became the mother of her first child, forever marked in her retina and heart, every second and every detail of that rainy and cold night of July 3rd, 1984, in the old maternity ward of the Guillermo Grant Benavente Regional Hospital of Concepción.

He was a baby conceived with great passion and a love overflowing with youth, the product of her first and grand love, who was born prematurely, but equally yearned for. Apollo made his entrance into this world as a great warrior god, fighting for his life and being born to protect the life of all humanity and ward off death. He was born in the midst of an atmosphere that a horror and suspense film, with the medical staff succumbing to the nervousness and mass hysteria that had been unleashed, not only in the delivery room but throughout the maternity and neonatal unit of the old Concepción hospital. The diagnosis was that Apollo had been born with his intestine outside his little body, which in medical terms is called Gastroschisis, it's a birth defect in the abdominal wall where the baby's intestines exit the body through a hole next to the navel; a one in a billion case and it had happened to them, a young university couple with no health insurance and financial solvency to face such a complex and unusual congenital issue with which their first baby had been born. They had to be strong and fight for their son's life. The following day, while in full convalescence from childbirth, she requested to be discharged, under her responsibility, so she could be close to her baby. She needed to recover and be well to be of use and save her baby boy's life.

Esmeralda was very thin and suffered from severe malnutrition and anaemia that arose during pregnancy, due to an insufficient and poor quality diet, which added to the daily vomiting ever since her first day of pregnancy and which persisted until the day of delivery; they were uncontrollable and inexplicable nausea and vomiting, that usually occur in some women during the first trimester and not during the entire pregnancy, as had happened to Esmeralda. She found out the answeu that only after delivery, when the neonatologist told them that continuous vomiting during pregnancy was a characteristic symptom when the foetus presented some malformation or irregularity in the gestation process, the organism naturally generates rejection or may even provoke a spontaneous abortion, which fortunately did not happen in Esmeralda's case –adding– it is possible to detect the malformation through an ultrasound, but unfortunately in Esmeralda's case they only did one and it was likely that at that moment the baby was on his back or in a position that made it impossible to detect the birth defect or its sex. The neonatal professional emphasized breastfeeding, that it would be crucial to continue nursing him when he was discharged, to help him regain his immunity and facilitate healthy growth, reason why he recommended Esmeralda to breastfeed another baby from the neonatal service or any other baby whose mother did not have milk, in order to preserve her breast milk. Esmeralda thanked and accepted the doctor's recommendation. But when she got home, Mario explained another film-like way of preserving breast milk, since he strongly opposed to the possibility of her feeding another baby.

–You are not going to feed another baby with my son's milk, I will drink your milk daily so you don't dry up and you will be able to feed our son when he gets out of the hospital –Mario ordered energetically.

And so, every day when she woke up, in the middle of the afternoon and before going to sleep, Mario, just like a baby, would lie in bed next to Esmeralda and drink all the milk, emptying her sore, feverish breasts with cracked nipples; she had so much milk that it was extremely necessary for Mario to drink it, even though there were days when she would have preferred not to. Esmi every day had more and more milk, it was incredible how it leaked from her breasts, to the point that even when she lay in bed on her back, the milk squirted out like a water fountain in a square, and while Mario drank the milk from one breast, she had to cover the other to prevent it from continuing to flow out like a never ending spring.

As a result of this practice, Mario began to gain weight and looked robust like a baby with his pink cheeks and his shiny skin, amen as jokes were made regarding it in their tight knit circle of friends, who were aware of the strategy assumed by the couple in order to ensure breast milk for Apollo, for example, it was common for people to make jokes such as:

–Mario, do you want me to burp you? Come, my little baby, so I can burp you –his university friends would say. In any case, it wasn't a joke, breast milk made him burp just like a baby.

On one occasion, perhaps for Easter, Esmeralda and Mario went on a weekend trip to a cabin in the mountains with a group of university friends; she accepted the invitation with the promise that the next day they would get up early to go to the hospital to visit her son and bump milk to leave at the hospital, since Apollo was tube-fed with his mother's milk. He started by consuming two cubic centimetres every two hours and slowly they increased the dose.

That night, while everyone was around the fireplace singing to the sound of a couple of guitars and sharing a pleasant evening, Esmeralda couldn't take it anymore with her sore and feverish breasts, so between laughs and jokes, she took Mario by the hand to go breastfeed him; when he returned everyone was laughing out loud and offering to burp him, but all in good vibes, everyone understood the situation while at the same time admiring the strategy they had adopted in order to maintain breast milk for the little baby.

The next morning, it was impossible to wake Mario up to return to Concepción from San Pedro, where they had been staying. No matter how much she shook him to wake up she couldn't, apparently, he had stayed up very late and had drunk way too much. Esmeralda went back alone to Concepción, heading down the railway in order to shorten her way on that cold wintery morning until she reached the train station. Upon arriving at the hospital, she ran into the doctor on call, who was making his morning rounds. When she asked about her son's health, he replied:

–Don't get your hopes up about your baby, you are a very young woman and you will be able to have all the children you want. Your son is seriously ill, he has undergone two operations and I don't think he will survive a third one. Be strong –the doctor concluded as he patted Esmeralda's back.

She began to cry, inconsolable, taking refuge in the neonatal hall, where she had to change her clothes before entering to visit her baby, and it was also the place where she pumped milk daily to deliver to the neonatal supply and feeding centre so they could feed Apollo. After going through her heart breaking pain receiving such discouraging and lapidary news, she walked slowly and almost without strength down the glass corridor, her gaze fixed on her son's incubator. Like every day, she caressed her baby over and over again by inserting one of her hands through the sleeves of the incubator, she told him stories and talked about the things they would do when he was discharged, they would go to the park and play, they would go to the countryside to visit his grandparents, swim at the beach and eat lots of ice cream and sweets, she also talked to him about when he grew up and went to school, how he would make friends until he became a great little man. However, that morning was very different, it was impossible to contain the sorrow and pain that invaded her; she avoided caressing him so as not to transmit her pain, because he could perceive it and that would negatively affect his delicate state of health. In that moment she felt a soft and warm hand on her shoulder radiating light and energy; it was one of the assistants that she saw daily and with whom she exchanged greetings and small talk.

–What's wrong, why are you crying inconsolably, dear Esmeralda? –she asked in a soft and understanding tone as she moved her away from the incubator and hugged her with infinite tenderness, as if she were her daughter or a loved one.

–My dear, calm down, don't cry; tell me what's going on now?

Esmeralda began to cry once again as she told her that the doctor had just informed her that her son wouldn't be able to withstand a third surgery, that he was too weak, and not to get her hopes up about the baby.

–Dear, listen to me, I've been working at this hospital for many years and have seen that sometimes doctors make mistakes, they give up on some of our patients, but with faith in God and with their parent's infinite love, and especially with their mother's infinite love, children miraculously recover before the doctors' incredulous eyes. Yes, that's right, they recover and sooner than imagined. I advise you to continue visiting your child daily, coming to see him every day, once or twice, or as many times as you can, caress him, talk to him, convey your motherly love, your affection and your protection, tell him how much you love him and how important he is to you, trust in what I am telling you, have great faith that your little boy will recover.

The days passed and just like the paramedic assistant had warned her, Apollo survive a third and even a fourth surgery, until finally, when he achieved two kilos of weight and the full maturity of his lungs, he was discharged, after three months being subjected to intense treatments in addition to surgeries. He was precious like an angel and as small as a toy doll, he had exceeded his birth height and weight, although he was still extremely small compared to the expected parameters for a three-month-old baby, being classified as being in a state of malnutrition during his first years of life.

Returning to the plans to make a pause in her life, having everything almost ready and organized, except for the permission from her boss, to undertake her trip to the British capital in search of a breather from her exhausting life as a public functionary suffocated by the routine, she began to feel a little more relaxed when she was surprised with countless farewells organized by different groups of friends: they invited her to dinners, drinks and barbecues, she felt very loved and became a role model for many of them, who wanted to have the courage, independence and economic facilities to take a sabbatical year and go, like Esmeralda, and study English in another country in the world, not necessarily to London, since England was one of the most expensive tourist destinations, as well as the English courses. She had made her choice thinking about the connectivity with the rest of Europe, which would make it easier to take a trip to sightsee and learn, in addition to being the homeland country of the English language, but there was another powerful and hidden reason in her subconscious that she had considered at the time of making the decision whether to go to study in Canada, the USA, Australia or London, it was the possibility of reconnecting with that great passionate love that she had with Todd. But she had no contact with him, she had lost track of him after changing jobs, so going to England kept the illusion of being able to achieve that by being closer to him, living in the same country. The last goodbye was in Santiago, an unforgettable evening with her closest friends from her university years, some colleagues from previous jobs, cousins and part of her family, and for her it was very important to have her mother and her daughter Renata there.

Despite the fact that the flight had an eight-hour stop in São Paulo, in addition to having spent a night in an hotel after missing the connecting flight for being distracted, it was a very pleasant and fun trip, even flying in economy class; it turns out that, when resuming the flight to London, one of the stewardesses approached her and very kindly greeted her with extreme familiarity, asking her with a smile:

–Hello, you're Esmeralda, right?

–Yes, that's me, why? –she asked surprised and curious.

–Ah! It's good that I found you! So, you're going to study English in London?

–Yes, I'm going to London to study English –Esmeralda agreed growing curiosity and a faint smile.

–That's great, I'm glad, you're going to have a great time and so much fun, I can assure it. If you need anything just let me know, with confidence, I'll be happy to help you.

–Ah! Great, thank you very much! I would love to change seats if that is possible, I don't like sitting next to the bathroom, because of the smells and the noise from so many passengers that constantly use it and won't let me sleep –she said smiling and with a pleading tone.

–Mmmm, sorry, the plane is full, that's not possible, I'm really sorry, but I can bring you another blanket and pillow so you're more comfortable, would you like that?

–Yes, please –she responded happy and grateful. The beautiful and kind stewardess returned not only with the typical package of pillows and a blanket, but also carried an amenity kit, those they give you in business class containing toiletries and an eye mask to diminish the intensity of the lights as you sleep.

It was an extraordinary trip; she felt that the stewardess had liked her, and had made an effort to make her feel more comfortable. The strange thing was that she couldn't understand how she knew that she was going to London to study English, nor could she ask her, because it was very difficult to talk and listen to her as she was sitting in the second seat near the window in a row of four passengers, besides that, every time she approached she was like a flash, she would exchange a few words or just smilingly give her a gift and quickly leave, so much so that she found the situation very uncomfortable thinking about the passengers sitting next to her; so when she brought Esmeralda extra drinks and snacks, she would give some to the entire row, though not always. The passengers seemed very happy that Esmeralda was sitting next to them; and needless to say, when she attended to her at mealtime, she would offer her two servings and she have second helpings repeat as many times as she wanted; it was the same situation with the drinks, she gave her so many that she made a real collection of whisky and wine bottles, the small cute one-serving bottles they give you on flights. It goes without saying, after so much food and drink during the flight, she slept like an angel and she felt like the trip was extremely short. A few minutes after landing in London, the stewardess approached her to say goodbye, commenting that she was happy to have met her and to please send her regards to her mother, adding in a nostalgic tone:

–I miss her so much, we were such a great team and when she left the airline, I felt so sad –in that moment the intercom bell rang again, it was time to prepare for landing. The girl quickly said goodbye throwing a kiss with her hand and left almost running to get back to work without giving her time to say a single word, she only managed to raise her hand in a gesture of farewell and thanked her. It had been a real confusion of passengers, with the great luck that Esmeralda had the same name as the daughter of the stewardess' friend, and that she was going to London to study English. What a strange and blessed coincidence!

Upon arriving in London and as a typical provincial tourist who didn't know how to get to her destination, she took the easy route: she bought the study package with taxi service to the house and to the airport, honouring the popular saying "Juan Segura lived 100 years" meaning that if you play it safe, you will get good results. Jane, the owner of the house, was waiting for her, and said:

–I thought you were arriving yesterday, what happened?

–I'm sorry Jane. There was a delay of more than eight hours in the connecting flight at the airport in Guarulhos, Brazil, and amid so much waiting, when the flight finally took off, I missed it because I didn't hear the call, I was too far from the new assigned boarding gate, so they sent me to spend the night at a hotel and they re-embarked me today on the first flight in the morning.

–Ah, that's what happened! I was worried about you; I couldn't call your school because it was the weekend. But come, come in, let me take your luggage –and meanwhile she commented that the next day another student, from Brazil, would arrive.

–Ah! That's great, excellent news!

–Yes, it'll be great for both of you; you can accompany each other and go to school together.

–Yes, that's perfect, but how will we communicate if she speaks Portuguese and I Spanish?

–Well, that's the idea, that you both learn how to speak English and that you practice just like you're doing with me, you don't speak well, but you make yourself understood, that's how you start, take it easy.

–Wonderful, but we'll have separate rooms, right? Because I paid for an individual room, I'm not going to share a bedroom; I want a room all to myself.

–Yes, don't worry, I have two rooms in order to receive only two students, no more than that, and only women, I try to avoid receiving men, they go out every night, come home late and make a lot of noise, besides they're messy and dirty. No, thank you.

She gestured her to follow:

–Follow me, I'll show you to your room so you can get settled in –and started to go down a stairway that began in a square-type opening that was on the first floor, on a slope that made it seem as if it were a small wall; that's how Esmeralda encountered one of the first cultural differences between her country and England: they call it ground floor, to what for a Latino is the first floor, and the second floor turns out to be the first floor for the British, super weird. Same as in the USA, floor number thirteen doesn't exist; they skip it when numbering, from floor 12 they go to 14 for superstitious reasons and to ward off bad luck.

The room was spacious, although it was a bit difficult for her to be underground because of her anxiety and panic attacks due to claustrophobia, she was terrified just thinking that she could be trapped, but she was reassured when she saw that she had natural light and could hear and see the birds through a small barred windows along the top of the wall that overlooked a small inner courtyard. It was also reassuring to know that from the next day on she would be in the company of Karla, the student who was coming from São Paulo. The next morning, a beautiful and energetic young woman with long blonde hair and bright green eyes arrived, very cheerful, who after leaving her luggage asked Jane, the owner of the house, to explain how to get to the nearest underground train station, telling her that she would go to the Notting Hill carnival, as she had been told that it was a unique and wonderful show that she couldn't miss, that it was as big and fascinating as the carnival in Rio de Janeiro. She invited Esmeralda to accompany her, and from that moment they hit it off very well, they took the same path to school and together they lived many adventures, laughing at silly things and worrying about being home late and missing dinner.

Yes, the English people have rules and they are very strict with them, Jane was very nice and kind, although she was also very attached to her own rules and routines, she was extremely rigorous, she didn't mess around when it came to dinner time, dinner was at six o'clock in the afternoon and if they didn't arrive before eight at night, she would throw the food away because the smell bothered her when she was in bed, complaining that it woke her. It was evident that heating food in the microwave, in addition to generating odours, made noise, and that woke her up. The issue was that it was an unconventional type of house, her bedroom was like on a second floor to one side of the wall, it was like a kind of balcony opened to the ground floor, where practically everything was, the entrance to the house –where you had to take off your shoes before entering and put on others that were exclusive for indoor use, or simply walk barefoot– immediately after that was the kitchen, followed by the dining room and the living room, which was between the ground floor and her bedroom, the house was beautiful although not very functional due to the lack of privacy in her bedroom. After two weeks, Esmeralda had already commented at her school about her need of changing houses, in addition to the fact that she had discovered that the owner of the house was an alcoholic after noticing that two out of three bottles of exquisite Chilean wine that she had brought as gifts, or to enjoy on an important occasion such as national holidays or the New Year, had disappeared,

She was transferred to the home of Hepzibah, a very spiritual, maternal and incredibly generous Jamaican woman, divorced, with three children and three grandchildren, from whom she received much love, support and understanding. She practically became a part of the family and loved by everyone, it was common for her to be invited to family parties and events in which her daughters participated. For Halloween they invited her to a costume party, and when she returned home Hepzibah asked her:

–How was the party, did you have fun?

–Yes, I loved it, I had so much fun, and I loved seeing the big round beautiful bodies the women had, wide hips and slim doll-like waists, and I have none of that –she commented turning around and showing her bum while touching her pants.

–Naughty girls, hahhahaha!

Indeed, all the people who were at the party were mostly Jamaicans, very cheerful people and good at dancing, singing and making jokes. There was another situation with Hepzibah that caught her attention that made them both laugh a lot: every day she appeared with a new wig, of a different hairstyle, even a different colour, and she also loved to wear eye-catching hats and caps. This was another new aspect in

Esmeralda's life, sharing with people from different countries, becoming fascinated with their cultures and ways of life.

The first day of school, she started it with her new friend Karla, they walked for ten minutes, following Jane's directions, until reaching Hampstead station, where they had to look closely at which train to board to go in the right direction, because otherwise it would make a detour and take them somewhere else, which usually happens when you are distracted, because on the platform where they had to aboard, the same line that took them to school had two different routes: part of the route passes through the same stations and then deviates to absolutely opposite destinations, Hampstead being one of those stations where trains pass through the same ones and then make a detour in the direction of their final destination.

Westminster Abby with her friend Karla

Karla and Esmeralda, became truly good friends

and continue to be in touch until this day.

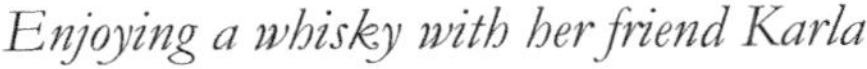
Enjoying a whisky with her friend Karla

When they arrived at school, they found a small waiting room packed with young students on their first day of class, just like Esmeralda and Karla. After checking their documents, the reception staff sent them to a room where they had to take a test to find out what level they were at. Karla was in an intermediate level while Esmeralda was in a pre-intermediate level, therefore each one was going to a different class. That didn't prevent them from walking to school together, at least on the way; sometimes on the way back it was different, because their classmates could organize different activities.

Upon arriving to the classroom, she found herself with about fifteen young students and a couple of adults, who were also students like her, with whom she quickly became friends. The age issue had never been a problem, it was indifferent, what determined her actions were her tastes and interests, regardless of age or what was conventional. If someone wants to do something and they can do it, without harming others, why not, that was the motto she lived by to act and enjoy her life.

From the beginning, the English classes were super weird, but also very interesting and entertaining. Yes, it was an adventure and she lived and enjoyed it as such, fifteen students equal to fifteen different countries, and not joking; that was how different the classes were. It was difficult and funny trying to understand each person's way of speaking, because regardless of whether everyone said Hello, everyone was heard differently due to the accent of their native language. They had to get used to it and tune their ear to understand what students from India, Portugal and Pakistan were saying because they sounded absolutely different, despite it being the same word or phrase.

Studying English in London

Being really bad at other languages, with an ear that couldn't be worse, her experience and way of seeing life helped her a lot; she took advantage of it, and took into consideration every message and recommendation she was given. For example, in school they were forbidden to speak in their native language, they had to practice and make an effort to take advantage of every instance of communication to speak English, even if it seemed very ridiculous to communicate in this language with a person from the same country, being able to do so fluently in their own language, otherwise they wouldn't learn to speak English. That's how Esmeralda always did it, even if she wasn't at school. Although there was a great age difference with the young students, who were mostly teenagers and at most some maybe twenty-five years old, they helped her a lot, they were equals, amen to the fact that she dressed similarly and looked extremely young for her age –she could easily pass for someone in her thirties, although she was close to fifty.

Studying English in London

Esmeralda made friends with great ease

She felt very comfortable and happy walking the streets of London thanks to the advice given to her by two key people; when she barely had time, she visited the Chilean embassy in order to introduce herself and volunteer as a social worker for whatever they needed, she had an interview with the Chancellor of the Consulate, a serious man, son of soldiers, very direct and frank to say things. In a very serious way and looking into her eyes, with a questioning tone asked her:

–Why have you come to London, to visit, to learn English, or in search of a British man to marry?

She was perplexed by the frankness and sharpness with which he approached her for answers, to which she responded, somewhat scared, yet convincing:

–To study English, of course.

–Well then, in that case, I will give you two words of advice, and please, do as I say, you won't regret it: first, don't do such a thing as to hang out with Chileans, you will not learn a single word of English with them, but you will have a good time, they will invite you to barbecues, to celebrate birthdays and there will be many, Chileans always find a reason to get together to eat and drink. The second thing, don't stay at home with the excuse that it's cold, go out anyway, and every day, it doesn't matter if it's cold, raining or snowing, just bundle up well, put on a wool hat, gloves and high socks, because I imagine you brought some, right? Because here you will need them, in winter it gets very cold.

They were words of wisdom that she followed to a tee. On the other hand, her friend Luis Silva, a Chilean man living in London since the late 70s, a lawyer who worked for an international charity organization, recommended her something similar, as they got together for coffee and she gave him an exquisite bottle of red wine of great reserve.

–You need to go out every single day while you're in England, even if it's raining, cold or snowing, you bundle up in warm clothes, prepare some scrumptious sandwiches and a thermos with hot coffee and walk around the streets of London; you can't miss this opportunity to go touring and sightseeing.

And that's how it was, every day after school she would leave with her classmates, with a friend or alone, using her school pass, she would take the train, get off at a different station and walk, getting lost in the old and cobbled streets of London.

She always toured around historic neighbourhoods, walked without a defined destination that took her to discover unthinkable places, photographing with her camera and her retina each of her conquests and discoveries. Her love and passion for Anglo-Saxon history led her to become a member of the museums and castles of the British monarchy, she had a free pass to enter as many times as she wanted, and thus she fell in love with the captivating and enigmatic Tower of London; she visited it countless times and always found something new and interesting that captured her attention, fascinated by its thousand and one stories, mysteries, its intrigues, deceptions, jealousy, weddings, wars, battles, plagues, famines, disloyalty, ambitions, trials, convictions. and beheadings, even of kings and queens, such as Anne Boleyn, the second wife of King Henry VIII, and Mary Stuart, the Queen of Scotland, who was beheaded after more than twenty years of captivity in the Tower. She hallucinated with the brilliance and exuberance of the royal crown jewels, kept in one of the Tower's dependencies, including the crown of the current

Queen Elizabeth II of England, which is fetched every time the queen requires it for a special ceremony, being returned to the Tower of London with great care and caution.

The classes were very entertaining and interesting; they taught English with material of the history of the United Kingdom and of interest to tourists, which captured their attention, this way they learned the language while soaking in the Anglo-Saxon history and culture, and also of the United States of America, Canada and Australia; the young students and Esmeralda, hallucinated with the behind-the-scenes of the formation and the breaking up of famous and consecrated rock bands, about the lives of artists and other celebrities; they valued shocking topics, like someone who had become a millionaire and famous in the blink of an eye with an invention or discovery, not always the product of work, effort and perseverance, but by accidentally mixing an ingredient or simply at random. It was fascinating to study topics like the beginning of Coca-Cola, McDonalds or Disney World. They also took into consideration social, cultural and entertainment activities, they even organized trips to tourist places in England and other European countries, being a great opportunity to venture with the support of the English school, go in the company of other students and at low prices. Ah! Something super cool was going to the bars with one of the teachers: the first day of class, which was actually every day Monday, a day in which new students arrived, as well as Fridays were the day of farewells, the teacher who was working that week invited the newly arrived students, and all those who wanted to be part of the adventure and fun, to visit a typical English bar or tavern. Esmeralda used to be the first to raise her hand and sign up, and that's how she got to know countless bars and the stories that were told around them, why they were famous and what personalities had visited them, there were a series of legends of love affairs and tragedies, duels for the love of a maiden, places where Britain's greatest betrayals and murders had occurred, reigns overthrown, and wars and battles won.

It was amazing. Esmeralda couldn't be happier enjoying her freedom after her blessed divorce. Although there was a situation that was unbearable not only for Esmeralda, but for other people as well, it was the unbearable smell of sweat that emanated from some students, they didn't know if it was because they didn't bathe or simply because they didn't use deodorant, or because of their type of diet, but the smell of sweat was nauseating and unbearable, even more so during the months of September and October, so much so that there were some days when it was hot like summertime and despite having the windows wide open, the horrible smell was intolerable, even though people finally end up getting used to it, like good animals of customs that we humans are. Of course, she tried to sit as far away as possible from those students, whether male or female.

Another very interesting aspect of Mondays, which was a real fascination for everyone, starting with the teacher, was the speaking class, where each student had to talk about what they had done during their weekend; it was a way of supporting and facilitating everyone to practice. In general, everyone stayed home with the excuse that it was very cold or that they didn't know anyone or where to go, that there was a language barrier, that they could get lost, that it was the first time they had left home, etc., etc. Without missing the pretext of not leaving the comfort and warmth of their bedroom, it was very rare for them to go out (well, it was the middle of winter and the temperatures were bordering below zero and with winds that rattled bones). On the other hand, Esmeralda was a boomerang of stories, anecdotes and adventures, everyone eagerly awaited her turn and listened to her fascinated, she always had a lot to say, and despite her poor level of English, she managed to make herself understood, using her hands like a real juggler to communicate through body language and inventing words, which caused everyone to loudly burst out laughing when listening to her; the professor was her great lifeline whenever she was stuck trying to explain something.

At All Ice Bar celebrating Esmeralda's birthday

Dancing in the So Ho nightclubs in London

Esmeralda was very sociable and a friend to everyone

There was a very good anecdote: among the friends that Esmeralda made during her six months studying in London was Isidora, a young Chilean lawyer who went to study English for three months as a strategy to get away from a suffocating relationship. Isi, was very nice, beautiful, very sure of herself. Her way of speaking caught Esmeralda's attention, she said a lot of gibberish, although they didn't sound grotesque coming from her. Isi would say to Esmeralda:

–What I like about you, Esmi, is that you're not even the slightest embarrassed to speak English, you're not the greatest at it but at least you speak it, I love that, that you dare to do it, even though you stink at it.

Graduation of her friend Isidora

Returning to the English class, when she tried to improvise by inventing words, the teacher would react:

–That word doesn't exist in English, Esmeralda, nice try –adding–: Spanish speaking students are known for inventing words, but no, keep delighting us with what you did during the weekend.

–On Saturday I got up very early and went to visit downtown London, it was really cold and there were few tourists walking in the streets, which was good for taking pictures; with respect to photography, I was in Kensington palace, yes, the palace where Lady Diana lived, in the palace there is an exhibition of her most beautiful dresses, which includes photographs of the ceremonies and opportunities in which she wore them, there are dresses and hats that perfectly combine, as well as purses and shoes, of extraordinary elegance and finesse, however what mostly caught my attention was her tenderness and love for children and her closeness to people. Such a pity that she died! –she sadly added.

An Italian classmate answered angrily:

–They killed her; she was assassinated by order of the queen.

–No, that's not true! It was an accident –the young girl from Taiwan intervened.

Everyone was speaking at the same time, all you could hear was "they killed her", "yes, they killed her because she was pregnant", "because she had given an interview discrediting the monarchy", etc. In that, the teacher intervened:

–Wow, this is great! I love hearing everyone speak, that's the idea, to generate dialogue. However, we must be cautious with our comments and opinions, no one knows exactly the cause of the accident and, there are several versions, although the death of Princess Diana was very unfortunate.

–Yes, it's very sad, I remember her lovely wedding, she looked beautiful, it was like a fairy tale, Esmeralda and other students added at the same time and sighing.

–Teacher, I too want to marry a prince, introduce me to one, please –a Caribbean girl exclaimed smiling and joking, causing everyone to laugh.

–Alright, Esmeralda, anything else you would like to tell us?

–Yes, yes, it turns out that I didn't know it was forbidden to take pictures, I was happy walking around the exhibition and taking photos until a curator at the exhibition approached me and told me in a serious and kind tone: "Please, pictures are not allowed", "oh, I'm sorry, I didn't know!", I replied and continued touring the exhibition. There were such beautiful dresses that I couldn't contain my desire and I discreetly took a couple of photographs, which I continued to do throughout the tour in each of the rooms, until I felt someone's presence, I felt observed, I looked to the sides, nothing out of the ordinary, and when I turn around, I saw a man in a black suit, headphones and white gloves, who looked at me very serious and frowning; perfectly understandable with just a look. I was about to open my backpack to put my camera away when I heard the guard's firm voice: "Please, madam, before putting your camera away, please erase all the photos you have taken in the palace", "What?", I exclaimed in shock, "Yes, you were warned that photography is prohibited and you persisted. Sorry". So, I had to erase all the photos I had taken inside Kensington Palace.

–Oh, what a pity! –all her classmates exclaimed sighing.

The teacher took the opportunity to advise them:

–It is important that all of you respect the British norms and rules, they are very strict in complying with them, you cannot break them, otherwise the same thing as Esmeralda or something worse can happen to all of you. Ah, and people caught taking something that doesn't belong to them can even be deported and banned from re-entering the United Kingdom.

To which a student responded:

–That's nothing, there are countries were they cut off people's hands when caught stealing.

–No, that's all made up.

–What, you don't believe it? Ask your classmates who come from Arab countries.

It was an incredible and astonishing enrichment of experiences and unique cultural learning.

Esmeralda noticed on her first day of school that there was a great rivalry between the English and the Americans as to how they speak English; Great Britain is the origin and homeland of true English, and that was what had motivated her to make the decision to study in London and not in another country. It was common to listen to teachers at every opportunity that was presented to them, and also to some English people, correct their students not only during class hours but also during break, in the corridors or living room, cafeteria or wherever they were:

–Excuse me, you don't say "vacation", you say "holidays". You don't say "elevator", the correct term is "lift".

And not to mention the pronunciation, which was absolutely different, although the spelling was the same, the pronunciation was completely different; these were some of the usual corrections:

–Pronounce them correctly; you say "tomato" not "tomeiro", "party" not "pary", "water" not "warer".

In short, there are countless differences between the English spoken in the United Kingdom and the one spoken in the USA, besides the differences depending on which area you live in, well, it's the same that happens in most countries, people who live in the south speak differently from those who live in the north, different customs and ways of life.

Another interesting debate topic, which came up with Esmeralda's intervention in one of Monday's conversation classes, was the way of relating to the British and discrimination.

Horse guards at Whitehall

As a result of Esmeralda sharing with everyone the pleasantly surprising experience she had during the weekend, something that broke with the stereotypical image of the English being frugal and cold people, it turned out that that morning she left home very interested in seeing the monument that had been built in honour of the women of World War II, called the Cenotaph, located near

Trafalgar Square. After having walked in circles without being able to find it, she approached one of the two guards who were guarding the entrance door at the Banqueting House in Whitehall, in front of the horse guard located in the Palace of Whitehall, that was the main residency of the English monarchs of London from 1530 until 1698, the year in which most of its structure was destroyed by a great fire; after this brief historical review that used to accompany each story, she began to tell with joy, euphoria and pride, that she had been treated like a true princess:

–Well, I was tired from walking so much and it was also very cold, since I couldn't find the monument to the women of World War II, I saw two guards guarding the Banqueting House, the one I had just visited the previous weekend, well, I walked over and asked him with an anguished and pleading face: "Hello, please, can you tell me how to get to The Cenotaph Memorial? I can't find it", the royal house guard looked at me smiling and very handsome and flirtatious, he replied: "Madam, The Cenotaph War Memorial is very close to here", he bowed, put a hand on his chest and with the other pointed in the direction and said: "I would love to have the honour and privilege of escorting you to the memorial, please take my arm", while looking at his partner and winking at him in male complicity. I couldn't believe what I was experiencing, that the guard had offered me, yes, me, to accompany me to the memorial, and not to mention walking together and holding his arm. I really couldn't believe it, well, what was I going to do, I accepted and smiling we left walking like a married couple, I laughed alone and he looked at me smiling and with a witty face. It was hard to believe, the monument was there, less than a block away from the Banqueting House, at that moment I was dying of embarrassment, my face was redder than a tomato, and he, letting go of my arm and bowing again said goodbye: "We have arrived, madam, this is The Cenotaph WWII Memorial, enjoy, goodbye, bye." And he left.

All her classmates were amazed and shocked with the experience she had lived, but not everyone had her luck, and thus many began to share their experiences.

–Because I'm from Colombia they discriminate against me, they think I'm a drug dealer.

–They discriminate against us because we come from Arab countries; they think we're all terrorists.

–When I ask for directions or where a certain place is, they don't even listen to me and they just keep walking.

–I don't understand why Esmeralda always gets treated nicely; she seems to flirt a lot –causing everyone to laugh.

The teacher intervened:

–Your experience was very interesting, Esmeralda, thank you for sharing and delivering so much tourist information and history of the UK and even with dates –but Esmeralda abruptly interrupted him:

–I just love the history of the United Kingdom and I'm fascinated by actually seeing what I read in books and encyclopaedias and, something that is happening to me now, is that every time I see a place in a movie where I've been to, I yell excited and, say to myself: I know that place, I've visited it, I've been there. For instance, the Windsor Palace, the Buckingham Palace, the Grand Bazaar in Istanbul, the Egyptian Pyramids... –another student added joking and with an incredulous tone:

–Yaaaa, and where haven't you been? Because it seems like you have travelled all over the world –and she responded laughing in the same ironic tone as him:

–And that's nothing; I'm just now starting to travel and getting to know the world, I'll take this opportunity to share with you one of my secrets, at least it is my way of touring: I never repeat any country or place, because I have no money, time or life to travel the whole world, so I'm not going to waste my time, my money and even less my life, visiting a place that I already know, I can return to the same country but to another part that I don't know, but, I insist, I prefer to go to another country because the culture is absolutely different, well, except for special exceptions in which I have to go back to the same place, such as to look for my swimsuit that I left at the hotel –she finished laughing, keeping the secret of her marvellous and magical little red shoes, which were the means to travel the world.

The marvellous and magical little red shoes

The teacher continued:

–Coming back to how the English are and the situations in which some of you have felt discriminated, it is important to keep in mind that, indeed, the English dislike being approached by a stranger on the street and even more so, if they do it inappropriately, it is super important to take into account, first of all, to say hello, apologize for stopping them and ask if you can request information, but what happens in real life, and generally it's young people who do it, is that they ask all at once "Hey! Where is the Cenotaph?" Do you think that if Esmeralda had asked the guard at the Banqueting House in that manner, that he would have been so kind to her and accompanied her to the memorial? Obviously not, with kindness and a smile we can go very far.

Ritual of the magical little red shoes

Esmeralda had visited the Grand Bazaar in Istanbul thanks to Saliha, a classmate, with whom she had become very good friends; he had invited her, along with another colleague from Japan, to spend a few days in Istanbul, the capital of Turkey, taking advantage of the long weekend when he would go visit his parents. Saliha prepared them before the trip regarding some customs that they had to respect at his house and during their stay in Turkey, such as wearing a turban when going out or when in front of his father. Saliha's mother was very kind to show them infinite amounts of turbans that they could choose from, and showed them how to properly wear it. His family was very welcoming and generous; upon arrival at the house, they were awaiting them with large quantities and varieties of dishes with typical foods from their rich gastronomic tradition. Saliha was an excellent guide. With his cousin David, who was also an English student, they took them to see the most classic places in Istanbul, visiting museums and mosques, where women couldn't enter, only men could enter barefoot to pray, and it was common to hear the Koran being recited through the loudspeakers, and seeing how at the sound of a bell, men quickly would close their businesses and offices and run to mosques to pray, then returned to their jobs; others would close the doors of their stores and kneel at the corner of the street to pray.

For her and her friend, the Grand Bazaar was a fascinating place, crowded with stores full of leather clothing, fabrics, wool, seeds, sweets, even animals, all wearing tunics and the women in turbans, it was just like what they saw in the movies, where a man in a turban leads you behind curtains and passageways until you reach the great caliph. Despite its great appeal to them, it also generated a certain degree of anxiety and fear. Ah, they also ran into snakes that danced to the sound of music coming from an instrument similar to the flute. There were glass pipes everywhere to smoke the steam of aromatic herbs, and obviously they had the pleasure of living the experience. Saliha's family didn't smoke, unlike the vast majority of Turkish people who did; they smoke a lot, one cigarette after another.

They took them on a catamaran ride through the river and were treated to an extraordinary number of Arab sweets, which Esmeralda liked very much; since Saliha's family wanted to meet them, they visited several houses of uncles and grandparents, who awaited them with warm greetings and abundant food. They had to enter barefoot and sit on the floor; only people who suffered from a serious health condition were exempted from that custom. Before returning, Saliha's mother gave them one of her turbans, which they could choose, and bags filled with Turkish sweets and chocolates.

Esmeralda was having fun in London like never before in her life, as the daughter of a very conservative and overprotective family. She was born and raised in the countryside along with her six family siblings, playing and helping out with the everyday jobs and chores. Being a young girl, she didn't miss the city as much as she missed the visit from her cousins, who travelled every year from Santiago, the capital of Chile, to the countryside, to enjoy their two months of holidays from school. There, more than twenty cousins got together, with whom she played day and night. In addition to helping with the harvest work, it was common to see them load trucks with watermelons and melons, shuck corn, being a part of the threshing and harvesting, helping to lock up the animals, and enjoying swimming in the river and lagoons. In general, what they did for fun was the active part of the harvesting work; what they saw as a game, for Esmeralda's father was help and relief, despite the fact that on more than one occasion they gave him a hard time breaking watermelons, running over crops, or driving horses away.

In London, Esmeralda sporadically and very punctually got acquainted with the colony of Chileans residing in the United Kingdom, thanks to the invitations that the Consulate of Chile sent her so she could take part in ceremonies such as a book launch, folkloric music concerts or the celebration of national holidays, moments that allowed her to meet and make Chileans friends. That's how she made many friends, among them Camila, a young girl, daughter of a Chilean woman and an English father, born and raised in England; she spoke very little Spanish and made an effort to practice whenever she had the chance to hang out with Chileans. She was a sociable person, with an eager personality, with extravagant ideas and a follower of trends and new projects, such as being part of the delegation project to planet Mars –she applied, but was disqualified in the third stage–; she was a lover of photography, a follower of Spencer Tunick and the royal family. Her status as a fan led her to live incredible experiences, such as getting up at three in the morning to be at a privileged location where the queen's carriage would pass, or on Christmas day to participate in the Holy Mass and manage to bring a bouquet of flowers and thus having the possibility of approaching a member of the royal family, which she achieved on more than one occasion, and to prove it she had a close-up photograph with prince Harry and William.

National holiday celebrations with Casa Chilena UK

For national holidays, she was invited to the September 18th celebration party that Casa Chilena UK organized each year, a civil society organization that brought together Chileans residing in the United Kingdom, with the goal of sharing their culture and traditions. They counted with the participation of the Chilean government authorities in the United Kingdom, such as the ambassador and consul and their wives.

This event allowed Esmeralda to meet and share with more compatriots and make new friends –executives and some young people, such as Macarena and Paulo, who invited her to continue celebrating the next day at a bar, with barbecue and dancing, in a more relaxed and informal way.

During the weekends, she would travel with her classmates to wonderful places in England, such as Stonehenge, the university cities of Oxford and Cambridge, Southend, among other places, and she was amazed by the vestiges of the Roman Empire culture present in ancient buildings, the museum and the extraordinary baths of the city of Bath in Somerset.

Esmeralda, honouring her zodiac sign and as a good Aquarian, loved water; but she was extremely disappointed with the beaches that she visited, with murky waters formed by a mixture of waters from the River Thames and the English Channel, with dirty sand made up of mostly mud than actual sand, and the famous low and high tide, that when she went to Southend she was impressed to find a desolate landscape, like a post-tsunami, with ships, boats and yachts stranded in the middle of the mud, and the water more than three hundred meters offshore, something unknown to her in northern Chile. Or Brighton beach, which regardless of being a beautiful seaside resort with a pier, entertainment, the typical waterfront full of restaurants and colourful shops for tourists, disappointed her, because instead of sand on the beach there were rocks, which caused her excruciating pain as she walked towards the edge of the water, which was a bit clearer and had calm waves, this depended on the time of year and the weather.

She spent her nights visiting bars and clubs, located on the streets of bohemian London; Soho and Piccadilly Circus were the centre of her ruin, where she danced until dawn, until she couldn't any more, along with her English classmates and tourists, everyone danced with everyone, it didn't matter who it was, that was the style, the idea was to have a good time.

Another interesting aspect of the English culture was that they share tables at bars, and it is common for two couples who don't know one another to sit at a table for four and place their own orders for food and drinks, although sometimes they exchange a little dialogue, usually related to the local service, and other times they even become friends.

At the end of November, she made a quick trip to Chile at the request of her ex-husband, who urgently needed her signature for the property sale of their conjugal society: nothing more and nothing less than the family home, an immense property with more than twenty-five rooms, a property that she never wanted despite being a wonderful house, with vitrified parquet floors, furniture with Carrara marble cover, a hall, living room, rooms on slopes, a fireplace, en suite bedrooms with exclusive bathrooms and even a jacuzzi, with floor-to-ceiling windows that allowed spectacular light and a unique view of the beautiful gardens and pool with waterfalls. Despite so much beauty she couldn't like it because she barely saw her children, it was so big and beautiful that it seemed like a museum to her; she remembered the trips to the beach house in Bahía Inglesa, where the family spent all day together, it was a small, comfortable and very cosy summer home, and what she loved was that there was only one television in the living room, which made it easier for the family to be together.

She made the rigorous signatures and after visiting her children and knowing that Victoria was fine, already living with her boyfriend and seeing her evident seven months of pregnancy, and visiting her parents, she immediately returned to London to continue her English classes, with the surprise that the English School would be closed for two weeks during the Christmas and New Year holidays. Everyone was excited and very anxious waiting for the day to travel home and enjoy Christmas and New Years with their family. Esmeralda had just returned from Chile and it was absurd to go there again, so she decided to take the opportunity to travel; she didn't have a specific place in mind, and that's how her magical little red shoes took her to Sharm-El-Sheikh in Egypt; she had never travelled to Egypt, and it was a great opportunity to get to know that country and get away from the cold winter of England. Upon arriving in Cairo, the travel agency was waiting for her at the airport, and she recognized some passengers from the same flight who were approaching the tour guide. After checking their vouchers, asking them to follow him to the parking lot and inviting them to get on the bus that was waiting for them, he introduced himself and kindly wanted to know:

–Those who speak Arabic raise your hand –followed by–: ok, now raise your hand if you speak English –and he added–: those are the two languages we will use to communicate throughout your stay on Sharm-El-Sheikh.

She, without speaking a single word of Arabic and only some English, timidly raised her hand, joining the English-speaking tourists. She began to feel a chill running down her back due to the fear and concern of being out of her comfort zone; she was sitting in the second row of the bus and addressed one of the couples sitting in the front row:

–Excuse me, please, can I go with you?

–Oh, yes, are you travelling alone?

–Yes, I'm travelling alone –she replied apologetic and crying out for protection.

–Don't worry, you can stay with us.

Esmeralda thanked them smiling and sighed in great relief.

When they arrived at the hotel reception, they said goodbye exchanging names and room numbers before anything else. In reality, she didn't need a babysitter or a bodyguard; she just needed to know someone was there in case of any casualties. The next day they greeted each other at breakfast and then she began her tour of the resort facilities to find out what extra services they offered and the travel possibilities she had, she wanted to see the famous Egyptian Pyramids; she was there and couldn't miss that opportunity, so she bought her ticket and took the flight to Cairo. It was Christmas Day and she wasn't feeling well, her health had deteriorated and she had a fever, they took her to the airport's emergency service where they injected her with penicillin before starting the tour of Cairo, on the way to the pyramids.

The tour guide was an extremely kind young woman that accompanied her throughout the trip, she even tried on two occasions to help her enter the pyramids, but it was impossible for her to go down more than three meters, because when she saw that the entrance was narrowing and the air grew thin, a feeling of claustrophobia overcame her, and she turned back. A very friendly tourist took her by the hand and said:

–Come with me, I'll take you, you have nothing to be afraid of, it's super easy to go down, really there's nothing to be afraid of. Where are you from?

–From Chile –she responded with a trembling voice while trying to gather the courage to go down to see the inside of the pyramids, she couldn't miss the opportunity after having travelled from so far away.

–You're from Chile? Ah, even more of a reason why you can't miss the opportunity to see the pyramids of Tutankhamun.

Saying this, he took her firmly by the hand and they began to descend a narrow inclined tunnel, where they had to crouch so as not to hit the top part. Although the tunnel was narrow, it was two-way, with tourists descending while others returning to the surface. After about five meters, she could no longer handle the anxiety and the suffocating sensation, she began to scream and asked Michael to let go of her and ran out of the narrow tunnel terrified, losing the chance to see the pyramids. She was left with only the pleasure of riding a camel and photographing herself in front of the most famous pyramids of Giza.

Enjoying Christmas time in Egypt

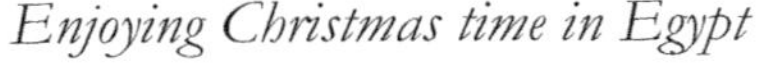

Enjoying Christmas time in Egypt

Afterwards they went to visit a town of craftsmen specialized in papyri, she was horrified by the filthy streets, which had become real garbage dumps and even with dead animals on the side of the road, the cars were very old and ancient, people looked very poor, wore long robes and the vast majority of women covered their hair. They travelled on tricycles, bicycles and motorcycles, there were very few cars and a couple of tourist buses and minivans. Upon returning to the hotel, an exquisite and abundant Christmas dinner awaited her in her room, and after eating it she went down to the resort's main hall to meet her new English friends, with whom she had shared her experience in Cairo. These friends told her that they had travelled to relax and support Estefanía, who had just lost her only three-year-old son to leukaemia.

Enjoying sailing in the Red Sea in Egypt

With more confidence, the next day they shared the whole day at the beach, enjoying the sun which was so elusive in England, and she enjoyed bathing for the first time in the Red Sea, she loved it for its crystal clear and warm waters, with waves and beaches of golden sands, nothing like the murky waters of Southend or Leigh-on-Sea in England and the rocky beaches of Brighton. The next tour, a camel safari through the Sharm-El-Sheikh Desert, included a telescopic view of the moon and an encounter show with the local culture, an occasion that allowed her to meet Keith, an Englishman of similar age, very friendly and nice with whom she formed a great friendship that would last a lifetime. It was a very warm day, the camel ride through the desert felt almost unbearable, animals that moved very slowly making the walk never ending. The desert was similar to the one of her beloved and endearing Atacama, although very dirty, with hills of trash, not only because of tourists passing by unaware and not at all friendly to the environment, but because of the clear evidence that people went to dump household garbage in the desert. While Esmeralda felt disappointed in the landscape, Keith complained that he couldn't sit well, that the camel's humps were too close together, that the space was very small and uncomfortable to sit and even more so the movement of the camel as it walked, which despite doing it very slowly, generated great pain in that particular part of Keith's body, it was too narrow for a person of his physical build, for a tall and stocky man; when he got off the camel he gave a sigh of great relief; meanwhile, her sigh was for getting down and being able to cool off and walk. They agreed with looks and laughter that the experience had been unpleasant and that it was finally over.

Esmeralda enjoying her freedom

Since they both came from England and were travelling alone, they teamed up, participating in the fire ceremony, dances and the preparation of omelettes, waiting for it to get dark enough to have a better view of the moon. They went out for a walk in the desert in the middle of the dark, the sky covered with bright stars, meeting about three hundred meters away two young experts in astronomy, equipped with two immense telescopes located in the direction of the moon, an image that reminded Esmeralda of the encyclopaedias.

Your new friend Keith

Looking at the moon was striking, amazing and very emotional; it seemed real and artificial and with a view so close that you wanted to touch it with your hands. There were many tourists and the stay in the desert was long, so she decided to sit down with Keith to talk about the tour and various other topics about England. The night flew by, when they realized that there were very few tourists left, they quickly got up and returned to the bus area without finding the bus that had taken them. It had left! Yes, they had left, leaving them abandoned in the middle of the desert. The few remaining buses also had left and only two remained, they felt the cold of the pampas and were terrified by the fear of feeling abandoned in a place completely unknown to them and with zero possibilities of telephone communication. They approached the guides asking about their bus and if they could please take them back at least to the city. Fortunately, the guides had two free seats, and they agreed to take them to their resort, Keith and Esmeralda couldn't believe the nightmare they were living, besides the cold that was beginning to seep into their bones, they were furious at the guide's irresponsibility, as they wondered:

–How did they not notice that two passengers were missing on the bus?

–It's impossible and unforgiveable that they didn't notice that two passengers were missing before embarking on the return trip. It's obvious that they must count the number of people and verify that they're all there, and if one is missing, they have to wait or go look for them, I can't believe they left us stranded in the middle of the desert, –Keith commented furiously, threatening to report the travel agency and discredit it as much as possible through its website and social media.

It was a horrific night, a few minutes before reaching the city, the bus driver stopped due to the change of lights a car made going in the opposite direction, a person quickly got out and asked if they were bringing two of their passengers by any chance, it was the tour guide who had left them abandoned in the middle of the desert. When Esmeralda and Keith recognized her, they got out furious and reproached the guide's attitude, and she in turn replied that it was their responsibility to return to the bus on time.

Back in London, Esmeralda was fully enjoying her freedom and stay in the British capital, attending her English classes daily and not necessarily studying, because once she left school the fun began; she resumed her role as a tourist, she visited palaces and castles and her great fascination, the Tower of London, which she had visited on countless occasions and which had left her with the desire to return once more. The history and art museums were another of her great interests; she visited them on those unbearable days of cold, hating the wind that seemed to sweep her away like Mary Poppins.

Another friend was Zoe, who invited her to Wales to spend the New Year at her mother's house, Rosa Betts, a chance for her to get to know the English social clubs. Those were community type venues, where members had access to various free benefits or for a very low price, such as musical events, dance parties, quiz nights, soccer games or dinners, although one of the most attractive aspects for members was the bar at almost cost prices.

With Rosa Betts in Wales

She enjoyed a spectacular New Year's night, shared with families of Chileans married to English in an environment of festivities, with costumes, and for the first time she was able to participate in person singing the traditional Scottish farewell song that gave her goose bumps, called "Auld Lang Syne", which they usually sang at midnight to say goodbye to the old year and receive the blessings of the new year, all holding hands and arms intertwined in a circle, that song had always moved her and caused her a great feeling of love and fraternity. She had the great opportunity to be part of this tradition, and better yet, to release Chinese paper lanterns into the air with a lit candle inside and a slip of paper with good wishes for the New Year.

Before returning to London, her friend Zoe invited her to Liverpool to enjoy the culture of the Beatles, touring the streets, the museum and the tourist tavern The Cavern, where the mythical rock band took its first steps to fame. It was an unforgettable night, drinking whisky and dancing to the music of the legendary English rock-band performed by a tribute band, which made it spectacular.

One morning at the end of January, with only six weeks left to finish her adventure, she began another very special one that wasn't in her plans, which turned her life 180 degrees. It was all due to the fact that her friend Luzia, a woman in her sixties –she was easily 58 –, Brazilian, a science teacher, that had travelled to London to learn English as part of her doctoral study curriculum, and with whom she had established a very close friendship, that day she arrived late to class and when entering the classroom, everyone stared at her in amazement without being able to take their eyes off her, she was dressed differently, she looked radiant, smiling and her eyes shining so bright that it could be seen clearly through her glasses, she walked in like a diva, like the owner of the place, wearing a beautiful and elegant black dress, pantyhose, high heels and she had changed her backpack for a black patent leather purse. When sitting next to Esmeralda, this one couldn't contain her curiosity and asked:

–Wow! And this change of look? Tell me about it! What's the deal? Do you have a meeting or are you going to a ceremony?

–I have a date, I'll tell you during break –she responded with a firm and defiant tone, like a diva.

Both Esmeralda and the students sitting around heard her say "date", and in unison they exclaimed:

–What?

It was just that her change was so evident when seeing her dressed so elegantly compared to how she usually did, like all the students, with jeans and sneakers, that even the teacher didn't resist the curiosity, in addition to the students discreetly commenting, making it almost impossible for him to continue explaining the use of prepositions. He cleared his throat to call attention and addressed his student and in a very diplomatic way began investigating the reason for such elegance:

–Luzia, congratulations, you look very elegant and stunning.

–Thank you, professor.

–I imagine you have a very important meeting by the way you're dressed.

–Yes, indeed, I have something very important to do today, but it's not exactly a meeting.

–Ah, a job interview, that's great, good luck and congratulations...

–Luzia abruptly interrupted the teacher and like an ostrich that raises its head and stretches its neck, with the voice of an empowered and very happy woman she clarified:

–I have a date!

–A date? And how is that? Sorry, sorry, forgive me for asking –while all the students joined in asking questions and murmuring in astonishment, the teacher turned around to the blackboard with a marker in hand saying: "Let's see where were we, that love... is a unique feeling...

And they all burst out laughing. As the class continued, Esmeralda and Luzia eagerly looked at the hands of the large clock on the wall, wishing it would move faster than normal, for a chance to talk.

When they were finally alone, Luzia told her that she had signed up on a blind dating website and that she would meet the person today at the National Art Gallery, located in Trafalgar Square. Esmeralda, very surprised, replied with fear:

–But how? Aren't you scared? He could be a psychopath and who knows what he can do to you.

–Calm down my friend, that's why I asked him if we could meet at the art gallery, because it's a public place and besides the security guards there are surveillance cameras everywhere.

–Ah, that's good, yes, that's a good idea, although I'd be really scared.

–No, there's nothing to worry about, if I don't like him then goodbye and period.

–Yeah, you're right. But how did you both get in contact? Tell me, tell me...

–Super easy, you go on the Internet and Google blind dates, there are many pages, I'm on Soul Mates, you could sign up as well, and who knows if perhaps you'll meet your XXI century prince?

–Are you crazy, no, I'd be embarrassed and scared!

–Embarrassed? Embarrassed about what if you're not going to do anything bad?

–Embarrassed that someone who knows me will see my name on those pages, what are they going to say about me, no, I can't, I am a public person in Chile, many people know me and in Copiapó I appear in the newspapers and on the radio, even on TV every now and then, no, no, that's not for me.

–Alright, you know what you're doing. In any case you could think about it, no one here knows who you are.

It was time to return to class, Luzia said goodbye with an air of fresh flirtation on her way to her date while Esmeralda returned to the classroom, but first she wished her the best of luck and asked her to take care of herself, and reminded her to call when the date was over to tell her all about it. When she returned to class, it was inevitable to gossip with her classmates about Luzia's date, everyone wanted to know, including the teacher.

Luzia called her without the enthusiasm with which she had seen her arrive at school. She told her that yes, she had met with her blind date, that he looked like an interesting, serious, formal man, but he had something that she didn't like, she didn't know what it was, it made her suspicious and mistrustful, and that she had decided to continue messaging him but that she didn't think they would go out again. Meanwhile, Esmeralda thought about what it would be like if she tried, in the end, no one knew her in England and there was so little time left before she had to return to Chile, she had nothing to lose in trying.

With Isabel and Luzia in the Underground

When she got home, she told Hepzibah about the blind date that her friend Luzia had gone on and that she was thinking about trying it for fun and her friend replied:

–If you want, I can show you the website I'm subscribed to.

–Ah! You're on those blind dating websites as well?

–Yes, why not? But it hasn't gone well for me, I haven't had any luck, I've been on it for more than three years and still haven't gone on a date, nothing, nothing at all, the men who have messaged me are old, fat and ugly –she chuckled and invited her to see her page on the computer that was on a small table in the corner of the living room.

The page was called "Plenty of fish". After seeing how it worked, she went to her room and began to fill out the registration form. She did it quickly and very naturally, answering with absolute truth and posting a very nice picture that she had taken on a canoe on a trip to Cambridge.

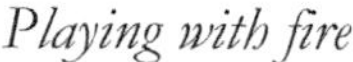

The next day, when she woke up and turned on her computer, she had hundreds of messages, she couldn't believe it, she was euphoric, she began to read and respond to the messages of the people that most caught her attention. She spent a week like that, smiling and jumping like a teenager from all the compliments she received, until she began to think about what her friend Luis had told her regarding blind dating sites:

–I'm registered on one, however, it's a waste of time, they message you saying that they are the sweetest women in the world, beautiful, without children, single, that they are young and that they have had bad luck in love.

–But yeah, it could be true, why do you doubt it?

–Because anyone can say those things, they write wonderful things and invent a colourful story or even better, they present themselves like Cinderella

–So then why are you still subscribed, if you know that it's not a good option and that you're wasting time?

–I'm still registered, because when I find an interesting profile, I immediately propose going out and I invite her for coffee or a drink, to see how real what they write is and quickly answer my doubts so I don't waste my time.

–Ah! That's a good idea!

–I have come across many freaks, they send me pictures of when they were young and on top of that photoshopped, and in real life they are uglier than a monkey and older than black thread.

That's how, with Luis's comment in mind, she began to ask out the prospects that most caught her attention, very handsome men, wonderful..., however, she always managed to find a "but" to avoid getting together, she would say as an excuse that she lived very far away and it was impossible to meet, even though they would even offer to receive her at their homes, no, she would never travel to Scotland, Belfast, not even to Liverpool, which was closer to London, to meet a stranger, no, how dangerous!, she would tell herself. She decided to lower the search level, put aside the profiles of super handsome men because she viewed them with distrust; they seemed a bit narcissistic and perhaps even gigolos.

In that, she came across Terry's profile, an ordinary man, with a normal profile. She disliked the fact that he liked cats and rock, as she was allergic to cats and hated rock, but something attracted her to him, perhaps the way he looked in his profile picture. There would be two complex issues to deal with, but she decided to contact him, in the end she had nothing to lose, it would only be to share if he were to reply and set up a date, they weren't going to start dating, much less marry. Determined, she sent him an emoji of a happy face, as simple as that. He responded after a few hours, they exchanged messages for three days, finding out a little more about each other, until she, following her friend Luis' advice, proposed getting together, which yes, she was interested in meeting him. They agreed to meet at the Embankment station, she felt extremely nervous and scared, but she remembered Luzia, there was no need to fear, they would meet in a public place and she wouldn't have to agree on doing anything she didn't want.

It was very easy for them to meet, he was waiting for her at the exit of the ticket barriers, they greeted each other and he invited her to visit his workplace. He worked as a maintenance engineer in the houses of the British Parliament, they walked through the beautiful gardens adjacent to the River Thames, from the Embankment station to Westminster, called White Hall Garden; they were wonderful meadows where she hadn't been, despite being so curious and having visited the area countless times. They both seemed nervous and talked very little; he seemed rather shy, so Esmeralda tried to talk, saying single sentences:

–Oh, what beautiful gardens, I have never been here.

–Yes, they are beautiful. I knew you would like it.

–Yes, I love it, the flowers are gorgeous.

–That's why I asked if we could meet at this station, so we had the chance to walk to my job.

–Ah, thank you very much!

That was the kind of conversation they had. When they reached the entrance of the building located in front of the British Parliament, called Portcullis, he stopped, indicating that this was the entrance. She saw in front of her an imposing revolving door of armoured glass and a few guards and policemen standing there even holding machine guns; Terry presented his identification card and informed that he would enter with his friend:

–Please, you must show them your I.D. card and they will search your backpack –Terry commented outlining a nervous smile.

–Ok –she opened her backpack, took out her student I.D. card and handed it to the guard, who after checking the name and looking at the picture verifying that it did indeed belong to her, he asked to check her backpack; he did a quick check and then ran it through the metal detector, but it made such a noise that everyone was alarmed and even the policemen put their hands on their weapons. Esmeralda got scared and asked Terry:

–What's happening?

–I don't know, they've detected something in your backpack.

–But, what? I don't have a gun or a bomb, what's going on?

–Don't worry, stay calm –he tried to calm her, but his face also reflected obvious nervousness and concern.

The policewoman took the backpack and one by one took out books, pencils, makeup, a bottle of water, a thermos, chocolates, creams and an infinity of things that women usually carry in their purses. She was flushed with embarrassment and very uncomfortable. When the police opened the other compartment, she took out a couple of plastic snack trays, and inside one of them was a metal knife and fork. That had been the reason for the alarm going off.

She breathed in relief, although she was still embarrassed, they requisitioned her and checked the backpack again. Since it didn't make any noise, they asked her to spread her arms and feet apart to do a personal check, just like at airports, but at that moment she could no longer keep it together and she asked very annoyed and angry:

–Why are you doing this to me? I'm not a criminal! –while the policewoman looked at Terry in search of an explanation and asking him what quality of guest he was trying to enter into Parliament.

He, very nervous, replied to the police that everything was fine, that she was Chilean and that she didn't know the rules for entering the building, while at the same time looking at Esmeralda and asking her with his eyes to be more friendly with the police, that they were only doing their job. Esmeralda became more annoyed with every minute that passed, they made her take off her raincoat, jacket, hat, gloves and even boots, they did an exhaustive check on her, besides feeling very intimidated when she had to turn around with arms and legs spread apart while Terry watched her, delighting in her graceful and proportionate figure. What a great embarrassment!

After all that was over, he apologized to her, but she was so upset that she felt like she was exploding and just wanted to go home.

With the sweetness and patience with which Terry spoke to her, she managed to calm down as they walked down a long and majestic ancient looking corridor, he explained that the corridor would lead them to the great hall of Parliament, and to the two chambers, the House of Commons –for MPs, Members of Parliament –and the House of Lords; she was enraptured by the majesty of the building, walking through an immense hall with statues of ministers and kings, it was really fascinating. Finally, he invited her for a drink at one of the many bars that were in the two houses of Parliament, something unusual and unthinkable for Chilean culture –Can English people drink while they are at work? –she asked him with extreme astonishment, and he naturally answered:

–Yes, why not?

–In my country that's impossible, in fact, there's an anti-alcohol law, they randomly test workers before entering their mining operations, and if anyone is detected with signs of having had a drink during the last 24 hours, they are sanctioned and can be fired from their job.

Laughing, Terry replied:

–Luckily, we're not in Chile, although I don't drink at my job, but sometimes when we leave, we get together at one of the bars, being common to run into one of the MPs and even the prime minister. I've never run into the prime minister, but I have run into several parliamentarians; the lords and the prime minister have other bars and restaurants that we cannot access.

–Really? Oh, that's interesting.

They entered a very elegant bar, located inside one of the two houses of the British Parliament, he asked her what she wanted to drink and she responded modestly that an orange juice. She didn't want to make it known that she loved to drink and even less whisky, she wanted to show herself as a lady with good manners and maintain her composure.

The bar had a spectacular view of Parliament Square, from where it was also possible to see Westminster Abbey and the noisy and bright city of London at night, with never ending traffic of red buses, so typical of England. Everything was going well, despite several events that caught her attention, the first and most unpleasant was being searched at the building entrance, something absolutely necessary and that she hadn't considered; then several people greeted him at the bar and, lastly, he showed her the profile picture where she looks radiant dressed in an orange suit and sitting in a canoe on the Cam channel, Terry, pointing at the picture with his hand, said:

–You're married; you have a ring on the ring finger of your left hand.

–No, I'm not married; I've been separated now for a few years.

–But, how, if you're wearing a married woman's ring?

Smiling she answered:

– In Chile we can wear rings on all our fingers if we want, it isn't necessarily a sign that you are married, in fact, look, I wear three rings, one on each ring finger and one on another finger.

They enjoyed each other's company, and this turned out to be a very successful and even fascinating blind date, except for the embarrassing incident upon entering the building. She was delighted with her first blind date, Terry looked like a good guy, shy, a nice person and very calm. She loved that he was chivalrous with her and had been fascinated by the idea of him taking her to see his workplace.

They said goodbye at the entrance of the train station, agreeing to see each other again, which they did a week later after work; on that occasion he invited her to dinner at a Thai food restaurant, they talked in a more relaxed way about family, jobs, tastes, interests and obviously Esmeralda's anecdotes and adventures in London, they laughed a lot while having an excellent evening. They agreed to go to see Windsor Castle the following weekend.

Romantic and classical music were a great delight and opera her passion, before travelling to England she dreamt of going to the Royal Opera, but it was a dream that she couldn't fulfil because the tickets were sold months in advance and were extremely expensive for those who weren't members or a part of the theatre's circle of friends, and the available tickets were with partial vision, she wasn't willing to pay a fortune to have a bad seat. That is why she had to settle with enjoying the classic musicals that were on the billboards throughout the year in London and for decades, she recalled that with her Brazilian friend Karla and cousin Flavio they had gone to see "Mamma Mia", they loved it, singing and dancing to the rhythm of the ABBA group, also doing mischief such as managing to change seats to other ones closer to the stage and taking pictures, which was forbidden.

Later, she went to see the musicals of "Les Miserables" and "The Lion King". Another extraordinary situation happened as a result of having met Terry, her new friend, who sent her a message inviting her to a rock concert at Wembley Arena, it was a heavy metal band called Rammstein, which she had never heard of until then. That invitation didn't attract her attention at all, and after a couple of days, he called her to ask if she was going to go with him to the rock concert, she answered hesitantly:

–Mmm, I don't know, to be honest –and she added raising her voice–: I can't stand rock music, I'm more of a romantic music type of person, ballads and blues, and I'm fascinated by opera. Not rock, sorry.

–Ah, I understand, but have you ever been to a rock concert? Have you seen a rock band?

–No, never, because I don't like rock music, I can't stand it, I'm sorry.

–What a shame, but I would like to see you anyway.

–Alright...let me think about it, I'll give you my answer tomorrow.

She thought about what she would do at a rock concert, she couldn't stand those type of people, wearing all black, leather jackets, tattoos, long hair, or with their hair standing up like porcupines, full of chains and with military-type boots, no, it was definitely not her scene.

While trying to decide what to do, she received a message from her daughter Renata, and took the opportunity to tell her about the invitation to the Rammstein rock concert. Her daughter, who was a rock music lover, responded very enthusiastically, and so loud that everyone in the house could hear her:

–What? you were invited to a Rammstein concert? I want to go! Please, please, I love Rammstein!

–Then go, I'll give you, my ticket.

–No, mum, seriously, it's a heavy metal rock band, it's a very famous German band. I would love to see them play.

–But what do you think, should I go or not?

–No, don't go, how dare you think that, you're not going to like it, even less you who loves music like Il Divo and romantic music, you even like opera, hahahaha, no, don't go, you're not going to like it, on the contrary I would happily like to go. But I can't.

The next day, ignoring the conversation she had with her daughter Renata, she replied to Terry that yes, she would go to the rock concert, adding:

–And, if I don't like it, well at least there will be the chance for me to leave.

In the end it turned out to be a fascinating, extraordinary, delirious experience, which to this day she says was the most extraordinary concert she had the privilege of going to, she was fascinated, blown away, euphoric, with the vocalist of the band's guttural voice, Till Lindemann, not to mention the special effects and the show, really extraordinary, with flames of real fire, you could feel the atmosphere heating up.

And when the vocalist got on a black Soviet-type inflatable boat and all the fans standing in the middle of the concert hall began to move it with their hands, moving him from the stage around the room and back! It was unbelievable. The special effects, the show, everything, it was wonderful. She spent weeks talking about the great experience she had lived, the beginning of her taste in rock music in her 50's. However, that night she wasn't able to sleep with the buzzing noise left in her ears due to the music, which lasted almost a week.

Rammstein concert

Among her classmates was a compatriot, Alejandro Meneses, a journalist from one of Chile's national television channels, who spent a month at the school sharing her class. He asked her if he could interview her for a report that he was preparing for his television channel, to which she gladly agreed, as did two other Chilean students. That interview was broadcasted nationally, and was seen by friends, acquaintances and family, who annoyed her because of how famous she was becoming.

Report for TVN Chile

She also relaxed by walking through the beautiful parks and feeding the ducks, geese, and squirrels. She remembers that one day after leaving school she went to visit Green Park and forgot to bring peanuts to feed the squirrels. Going through her backpack she found chocolate, she opened it and it occurred to her to offer one of the squirrels a piece, they loved it and she gave it to them in tiny squares until they ate it all. When the chocolate was finished, she left and the squirrels followed her a few meters wanting more. Poor squirrels, they had enjoyed it and probably had later suffered a big stomach ache!

With only a month left to finish the course in London, Esmeralda stopped enjoying herself, her enthusiasm and overflowing happiness had faded, resembling the grey winter days typical of the British capital, covered with fog, short days and very cold. She couldn't sleep thinking about the possibility that her grandson would be born before the scheduled date, her daughter being a first timer and not being sure in which month she had become pregnant, because her menstrual cycle was not regular the date of delivery was more uncertain and her despair increased. That is why she decided to return early to Chile, she couldn't fail her daughter again, she would never forgive herself, least of all Victoria. She managed with the insurance company to change the return date on the ticket back to Chile; she had a very powerful reason: the birth of her first grandson.

Meanwhile Terry was writing and calling her more often and asking her out. She felt that he was becoming fond of her, but Esmeralda didn't have a new relationship in her plans, much less falling in love again and not to mention getting married, although a second marriage is better than the first, at least that's what she thought. She avoided going out with him and when she did, she tried to look as shabby as possible, she didn't put makeup on and she wore the clothes she liked the least and that didn't fit her too well. The day Terry went to pick her up in his car to go to Windsor Castle, she put on a pair of pants and a sweater that didn't match at all, and went to Hepzibah to ask her for her opinion.

–Hepzibah, what do you think of this outfit I'm wearing, how does it look?

–Mmmm, no, I don't like it, the flower print on your pants doesn't match the blue stripes on your shirt.

–Ok, ok, thank you –and she went to her room jumping like a little girl and singing, she changed again and asked Hepzibah for her opinion.

–Yes, that outfit looks better, although yellow and black don't really match.

–Ok, ok –and she went to change for a third time.

–No, impossible, that outfit truly looks bad; you look like a scarecrow, go and change before your lover arrives. Naughty girl.

–No, no, he's not my lover, he's just a friend, I don't want anything with him nor with anyone else, I'm happy being single and also you know that in a couple of days I have to return to Chile –she replied annoyed.

–But you can tell he likes you, he's crazy about you, yes, yes.

After a few minutes the doorbell rang and Esmeralda ran out of her room to say goodbye to Hepzibah, who was stunned to see how she was dressed. She raised her voice and angrily rebuked her:

–Esmeralda, you can't go out on the streets looking like that, you look horrible, go change, you look like a scarecrow –she ordered yelling as if she were her mother.

–That's what I wanted to hear, I look better than I thought, thank you, thank you, Hepzi, I love you, I'm happy, I look better than I thought –and she left blowing her kisses with her hand.

Terry greeted her smiling giving her a card, chocolates and flowers, it was Valentine's Day, and she was left plop! She had no idea it was Valentine's Day. The trip was quite uncomfortable because he seemed really interested in her, he tried to approach her and whenever he had the chance, he would put his hand on her shoulder or try to take her by the arm. They toured the majestic, pompous and beautiful Windsor Castle, dazzled and open-mouthed by the marvellous architecture, the brightness of the gold dust paintings on the ceiling of the different rooms, so many paintings and portraits of the royal family members of the English Empire from centuries ago, the armchairs, the curtains and the lamps, objects of such beauty that they were almost impossible to describe.

Back in London Terry didn't want to say goodbye to her, he took her to China Town to see the celebration of the Chinese New Year, an opportunity she had to relax while walking among the groups of gigantic dragons made of red, orange and green paper. Finally, they stopped for dinner at a restaurant as it was already dark.

Esmeralda asked him to take her back to the house and the way home seemed endless; there was great silence between them, he wanted something more and she only thought about returning to Chile, she didn't want to live an adventure of a couple of days, no, that didn't go with her. It wasn't a touch and go.

When they said goodbye, he tried to kiss her on the lips and she managed to avoid him, moved her face and evaded him. Esmeralda was a peasant woman, raised under great discipline and where love affairs didn't exist, where you were only supposed to have one partner for the rest of your life, marry as a virgin and be united forever. She had already failed once and was not willing to do it again.

The preparations for her return to Chile began and with them the farewells. She went to say goodbye to her great friend Bernardo, founder of the Hampstead Lions Club, who invited her to have an exquisite dinner with the president of the club and their respective wives; they thanked her for having had the initiative to join their club during her stay in London, being for both clubs, both the one she represented in Chile and Bernardo's, a great opportunity to meet and exchange experiences of the volunteer work they did in England and across the Atlantic.

Bernardo Stella

Her classmates and Hepzibah's family also organized farewell parties, delicious dinners, trips to the park and playing in the snow, and the inevitable goodbyes in her favourite pubs and bars, including a couple of nightclubs in Soho. She felt like a queen, she had a wonderful time; her trip to London had been a once in a lifetime experience that had turned her life upside down 180 degrees.

Her Friends Hepzibah and Elena

Terry kept courting her and didn't want to let her go without at least stealing a kiss; he was deeply in love with her. Two days before her trip, they agreed to meet at the same Embankment station where they had met for the first time; he invited her to a very special place, with which she fell really in love. It was a small boat anchored in the Thames, set up as a floating bar, with bars at the stern and bow, just in front of the London Eye, with a spectacular view. Inside, the bars and restaurants were very luxurious, on the ground floor there was a big nightclub and a theatre, she was fascinated and she was very sorry that there were only two days left before her trip; if she had seen it before, she would have surely become a regular customer.

Esmeralda shined with joy, sitting at a table next to the window that showed the best view of the London Eye, he on his part, looked very handsome, his blue eyes stood out with his shirt, even though it was the same colour. Both shared in a very pleasant way and she forgot at times to protect herself from him, in the sense of not giving him false hope.

The farewell was quite complex. First of all, Terry didn't want to leave the little boat trying to extend for as long as possible the moment to pour the last sip of beer, he was very aware that the train station was just a few steps away and it would be the last time he would see and enjoy her company, just as he would have the last chance to steal a kiss from her. When they left the bar, they walked very slowly, when they reached the ticket barrier, he took out his card and marked it and passed through, surprised she asked him:

–Why have you marked your card and entered the station, if this isn't your line?

He responded with a sad face:

–I'm going to drop you off; I'm going to take you to your house.

Esmeralda reacted sharply and replied almost rudely:

–No, no! Don't even think about it, it's not necessary! Besides, you live really far away from my house and this train is going in the opposite direction.

–Don't worry, I want to go with you, it's the last time that we will see each other, let me do it.

–I insist, it's not necessary –repeating–, this train is going the opposite direction from your house –they looked at each other knowing that they had no more time left and that it was time to say goodbye. Esmeralda, calmer, lowered her guard and hugged him goodbye, it was a big hug, with a lot of love and contained feelings, when she tried to move her arms away from him, he held her and then desperately looked for her mouth to kiss her, she managed to get away and she started going up the stairs towards the platform where she had to take the train back to her house, having then to go down two different stairways with an intermediate floor, she ran as if they were chasing her to kill her, with the luck that she managed to get on the train that was about to leave; he arrived when the train had already started, they looked at each other for the last time and said goodbye, gesturing with their hands, seeing how the tears rolled down his cheeks.

On Friday was her last class, the day on which she invited all her classmates to visit the bar on the little boat, there were more than thirty, all fascinated taking pictures in the bow and stern bars with views of the London Eye, then inside the boat, they ordered food to share and drank beers, and Esmeralda, as always, whisky. From the bar they went to the nightclub and had a very lively party, dancing as if the world was going to end. She was euphoric and didn't want to leave, until she had to say goodbye before the last train at 12:45 a.m., her clothes were wet with sweat from dancing, jumping and singing, she slept for a couple of hours and at 6 a.m. she was picked up and taken to the airport, like that she was ending her incredible six months of adventures, travel and fun in London as a student and more than anything as a tourist, a once in a lifetime and unforgettable experience that would accompany her for the rest of her life.

Enjoying London life

Tower Bridge

Telephone box and Big Ben

CHAPTER III

Welcome to reality and the world of a miner

As soon as the plane landed in Santiago, Chile, she activated her cell phone to call her friend Jessica, a long-life friend, whom she could trust and, indeed, she had entrusted the life and health of her daughter Victoria; anxiously and with heavy breathing she spoke to her:

–Dear friend...my friend...Jessica, it's me, Esmeralda, I've just landed in Chile, how's Victoria doing, was my little grandson born? – she said everything at once... so much was her desperation to be there on time and be with her daughter during that very special moment in her life, such as giving birth and becoming a mother; her friend happy and serene responded:

–Calm down, calm down, my dear friend, everything is fine.

–But tell me; tell me, please, has my little grandson been born, or not yet?

–Calm down, not yet. Yesterday I went to check up on Victoria, she's doing fine and her baby as well, in the correct birthing position, she's on the right date and it could be any minute now; I give her two days tops.

–Ah! That's great news, Jessica; you don't know how grateful I am! You have been a true angel; I don't know how to repay all the support you have given Victoria and I; I love you so much my dear friend.

–Don't worry about it, that's what we're here for, right? Alright, now tell me, when do you arrive in Copiapó?

–Today, as soon as I get off the plane and retrieve my luggage, I'll embark to Copiapó.

–Ah, great, we're expecting you; you know, you can go to my house whenever you want.

–Thank you very much, my dear friend, I thank you from the bottom of my heart.

–I'm so happy you made it on time; your daughter is going to be so happy and grateful. But how did you manage to do it, weren't you returning mid-March?

–I changed my ticket, Jessica; I couldn't stay in London any longer, I was dying of anxiety and anguish. Also, you know the circumstances in which Apollo was born, I hope to God that Victoria has a normal delivery and that everything goes well.

–Yes, stay calm; the baby looked fine on the ultrasound.

–I have to go now, I'm getting off, see you later. I love you, my friend.

–Have a nice trip, Esmeralda, I love you too.

For a change, another unforeseen event occurred: one of her suitcases, the largest one containing all the gifts and most valuable items –including her jewellery– was missing, she couldn't find it. She left it on record at the airline office and ran to embark for Copiapó, she couldn't wait and at that time, her luggage wasn't relevant.

Upon arriving in Copiapó and collecting her luggage, she took a taxi to Victoria's house. Her daughter was surprised to see her and greeted her coldly, just like her son-in-law. Esmeralda knew that she could be received with a cold and distant greeting, as if they were strangers, but she had deeply longed in her heart that it wouldn't be like that and, had prayed a lot to reach her little heart, trusting that during her pregnancy and living such a sublime and special period of her life carrying a child, perhaps she could receive her lovingly. Unfortunately, it wasn't like that and although it broke her heart, she had to stay strong and be useful. On the other hand, she was very aware, and for that she felt extremely guilty, that Victoria was very angry with her for having gone to London despite her pregnancy, and that her father would remind her of it every day and whenever possible, poisoning her heart and distancing her more and more from her mother; this damaged not only Esmeralda, who was his target, but also and at the same time, it psychologically destroyed Victoria, generating hatred towards her mother and unforgivably splitting the family apart.

That day she joined her to one of her last pregnancy check-ups and the next day, her grandson was born; her other great friend and midwife Cecilia Díaz and the anaesthetist, her friend jeepers Renato, were part of the medical team, while the gynaecologist was the father of one of Victoria's schoolmates. Everything took place in an environment of great familiarity, the delivery was very fast and everything went smoothly, although minutes before, Victoria's screams echoed through the old house of the Copiapó Clinic, until Renato came running preparing himself to place the epidural and soothe her pain. Her screams were shocking and, despite being in the delivery room and having the support of Vittorio and Esmeralda, she screamed at the top of her lungs:

–Ayyyy, ayyyy, it hurts so much, I can't stand it anymore!

–Calm down, my love, the doctor is here –Vittorio said taking her hand and caressing her face.

–It's just that my baby is going to fall, he's going to come out –Victoria yelled.

Her friend Cecilia, already dressed in her midwifery attire and a couple of assistants approached; Cecilia took Victoria's hand as they pushed the stretcher towards the delivery room, while she continued to scream due to the strong and unbearable pain of her contractions, repeating tirelessly:

–My baby is going to fall, he's coming out...he's coming...! I know, I know, I can feel him! –she screamed in desperation.

Cecilia, motherly and professional, spoke to her trying to calm her down as they hurried down the corridor to the delivery room. At that, Apollo and Renata along with their father came running into the waiting room, faces of joyful curiosity and wanting to know if the baby had already been born. Esmeralda hugged her children Renata and Apollo with great joy, saying:

–No, no, not yet, they've just taken Victoria to the delivery room!

–Ah, so we've arrived just in time!

–Yes, yes, that's great! –Renata exclaimed in relief.

Everyone was euphoric and very happy awaiting the arrival of the new family member. Esmeralda and Mario kindly and happily greeted each other like family, being one of the few times that they did. It was a great family event and everyone was together. And then, Renata asked a little worried and embarrassed:

–Mum, mum, is the smell of smoke and alcohol noticeable? We were at the beach having a barbecue, we didn't think Victoria would be in labour today; you had said that she still had two more days left.

–Don't worry, darling, the important thing is that you made it here on time and that we are all together.

Apollo added in a calm tone:

–What are you so worried about, forget it, the important thing is that we're all here for our sister and we're going to meet our nephew.

To which his father replied confidently relaxed:

–That's the way to talk, son, who cares if we smell like pisco –a typical Chilean grape brandy– and smoke, do you think they'll kick us out?

A few minutes later the doctor appeared with Vittorio, both dressed in hospital cap and gown, the doctor wearing green and Vittorio in light blue, who was carrying the baby in his arms, snuggled against his chest and very excited showed him while saying:

–My son was born, here he is, he is chubby, healthy and his name is Viccencito –the whole family rushed to see and touch him, Esmeralda placed her index finger in her little grandson's tiny fragile hand, who clung firmly on to hers, and in that precise moment a bond and a sublime love was born between her and her beloved grandson. Everyone was very happy seeing the baby, and the doctor explained:

–Congratulations, as you can see, the baby was born, everything was fast; it was a normal delivery without any casualties. Victoria is doing fine. The baby was born with weight and height above normal levels, making him a large and healthy baby.

Everyone thanked the doctor for his excellent work and for the great news he had just delivered. Addressing Vittorio, he ordered:

–It's time to take the baby back to his mother.

Everything was wonderful; Mario invited Esmeralda to join the celebration at the bar, which she happily accepted since it was a great opportunity to share with her children. Before leaving the hospital, her friend Cecilia pulled her aside, and gave her a big hug:

–My dear friend, it's so good to see you, I'm so happy I made it on time.

Esmeralda burst into tears of the emotion and gratitude telling her between sobs:

–Cecy, Cecy, my dear friend, you don't know how anguished I was, I didn't think I'd make it.

–But you made it, you're here, it's so good to see you, my friend, tell me, tell me, how was it?

–Super, super, everything was fascinating, you have to go to London, my friend, it's another world –becoming serious and looking at her with a pleading tone–: My friend, we'll talk about this later, Cecy, now it's time for my little grandson.

–Yes, of course, we'll talk later, but you have to tell me everything, everything, in great detail.

–Yes, of course –Esmeralda replied.

–Alright then, look, there's your little grandson, in his crib, do you want to hold him?

–Yes, yes! Can I?

–Of course, aren't you the grandmother? –she responded laughing while picking up the baby.

Esmeralda was overflowing with the happiness and excitement of having her little grandson in her arms for the first time, the fruit of her beloved daughter Victoria and an extension of her family. The baby held onto his grandmother's finger with an incredible firmness that shook Esmeralda's heart, tears rolled down her cheeks as she appreciated the beauty of her grandson, who still had his semi-wrinkled and bluish skin from having spent nine months floating in the ocean of love and life that his mother had built with so much care so that he could live and grow healthy, beautiful and intelligent.

From cloud nine which she was on, she heard Renata from a distance calling her:

–Mum, mum, we're leaving, are you coming with us?

–Yes, yes, I'm coming –she responded after giving Viccencito a kiss on his forehead, as a sign of blessing and goodbye, she handed him to Cecilia but not without first snuggling him one last time against her chest. She gratefully said goodbye to her friend promising to get together to talk about "the human and the divine", as Cecilia would say.

Sharing with her ex-husband and her children was very pleasant, they were all very happy, however, they didn't speak a single word about Esmeralda's trip or her return from London; it was a forbidden topic. That night she slept at her friend Jessica's house, and told her in great detail how the encounter with Victoria and the delivery had gone, as well as seeing her ex-husband, her son Apollo and Renata.

Jessica was tremendously glad to see Esmeralda so happy, she had seen her in so many situations of extreme sadness, distraught and about to die, that she had to treasure and make this moment of happiness last as long as she could, longing to forever see her as happy as she was. Jessica was very grateful, as was her husband Tito, for the crucial support that Esmeralda had given her after suffering a serious car accident, leaving her paraplegic and unable to walk for life; however, she was able to continue working, becoming very successful in her profession, reaching high positions at a work and union level, with postgraduate courses and even a couple of specialization scholarships abroad. They spent that night talking, catching up on everything that had happened during the time they hadn't seen each other.

Esmeralda fell into bed exhausted, falling prey to a deep sleep, from which she couldn't be awakened not even by the 8.8 magnitude earthquake that would hit Chile at around 3.34 am, the epicentre being in the Pacific coast in front of the Biobío region, causing great material loss and the death of more than five hundred people, which wasn't too many in comparison to the amount of deaths caused by the tsunami, a natural event that the authorities on duty didn't promptly alert, a tragic natural disaster known as F27.

Fortunately, the clinic where Victoria was at, had suffered minor damages and she and the baby were in perfect health, while everyone joked and laughed at the force with which Viccencito had arrived in this world, causing an earthquake of an 8.8 magnitude and a tsunami. Esmeralda began to play her role as a grandmother; she looked happy and very grateful to life and God for having had the possibility of being with Victoria at that special moment in her life and for having great friendships, which were very close during the pregnancy and the delivery. She advised and helped Victoria with the care of the baby, she explained and showed her how to pick him up, hold him in her arms and breastfeed him. Fortunately, Victoria had plenty of milk to feed her son, who didn't stop eating day and night; the days and months went by, she visited her daughter and little grandson every day, tightening each day the bond of infinite love between grandmother and grandson, not so much though with Victoria, who remained surly and distant.

Esmeralda manages to make it on time

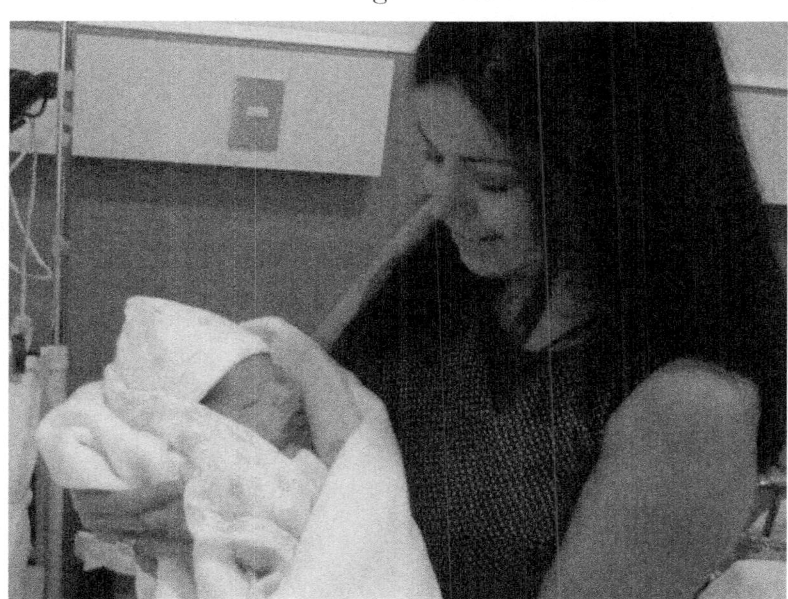

Esmeralda's return to Chile, to her job and to her normal life had been a very difficult process, with both of her houses rented out and unable to make use of them and finalize the lease contracts. That meant that she had to stay at her great and generous friend Jessica's house and later on, at Marcelita's house. As she had no job, it wasn't prudent to request one of the properties to live in, since that income was essential due to her unemployment. Illusive and naive like always, she thought that with the change of government, the removal of leaderships and trusted personnel of the outgoing authorities, it would be very easy for her to re-enter public service. It wasn't like that, and since she wasn't close to or active in any political party, the chances were almost nil, despite trying to be a part of and integrate into the political current of the moment.

She took advantage of the time while waiting for a good job opportunity, to study a postgraduate degree, returning to university life as a Master's in Business Administration, MBA student; it was an area that had always interested her due to her facility in mathematics and doing business, although her projects hadn't been entirely successful up to that point. Her return to university allowed her to reconnect with old friends and make new ones; she re-flourished and regained her charm, an opportunity that allowed her to be suggested by a fellow student to work in the private sector, not necessarily in her career as a social worker, but instead assuming the representation of a pharmaceutical chemical laboratory in northern Chile, a job that contemplated a medical line with dermatology products and a commercial area of social protection aimed at the work world, with a star product called Sunnywork, a successful business niche in response to the sun protection law that employers had to implement to protect the health of workers exposed to ultraviolet radiation, in order to avoid damage from sun exposure and reduce the risks of acquiring skin cancer.

That work experience was an excellent opening and a professional and personal growth, a great challenge in every aspect and, a professional specialization and field work; in addition to being her own boss as she was evaluated based on the sales levels she reached, on which her salary depended. In her new professional role, she underwent a radical change of wardrobe; she used to stand out for dressing with delicacy, finesse, elegance and formality, although she had to maintain that style when visiting dermatologists and pharmacies, being her fundamental role in the mining fields of medium and large mining companies, she was required to change from her two-piece suits, impeccable dresses and heels to jeans, a mining helmet, and safety boots. However, she maintained her elegance, delicate appearance and feminine personality, making herself noticeable wherever she went and, in particular when arriving at a mining, construction or service site. She didn't have a work schedule, it was customary to get up early and drive two or three hours until arriving to the mining site at the top of the mountain range to give an induction speech to the workers at seven and eight in the morning, before they started their work day, teaching and making them recommendations about sun protection, which had to be very enjoyable, precise, practical and at the top of her lungs.

In general, Esmeralda had to be ingenious and very astute so that the workers would listen to her and to capture their attention while she carried out her educational work in the field. She didn't always dispose of a room, a container or a warehouse where she could shelter from the cold or lethargic heat of the northern summer, improvising then a classroom between containers or warehouses that helped to block the mountain wind of the cold winter or reduce the devastating and implacable heat of the northern pampas, having to carry out her work many times in the middle of the pampas, hills and sometimes by the ocean or under vineyards. It was an adventurous and risky job, which she enjoyed because she was a lover of freedom and adrenaline. On the other hand, she would try to return home early so she could run to her daughter's house and enjoy her role as a grandmother, a role she played with admirable devotion. She fully gave herself in accompanying and helping her daughter Victoria with taking care of the baby, everything was new to Victoria, and as a first-timer, she was invaded by fears, anguish and thousands of questions, striving and staying awake to protect, care for and raise her baby, radiating an infinite motherly tenderness and love. Victoria, like her mother, turned out to be a very good milkmaid, she had so much milk that when she would finish breastfeeding her baby, the milk would continue coming out of her breasts as if nothing had happened.

Days and the months passed and Esmeralda felt more happy and proud every day seeing how her daughter had turned into a devoted mother and herself into a grandmother. She visited her daily, generating an indissoluble bond with her little grandson, diametrically opposed to her daughter Victoria, who was cold and distant towards Esmeralda, breaking her heart and, no matter how many times she tried, the therapies and medicines, there wasn't a way to restore that relationship between mother and daughter, which had been so close and wonderful during her childhood, to such an extent that Esmeralda's mother and her friends reproached her for showing a notorious preference for Victoria over her other two children. Victoria was very hurt by her mother, she would never forgive her for having separated from her father; her children didn't want to stay away from their father and, he as a strategy to keep Esmeralda at home and with him, would scare them by saying that their mother was crazy, that she had tried to commit suicide and that she was willing to do anything, that in a spur of madness she was even capable of killing herself and all three of them together, in a simple act such as crashing the car into a train or flying into a ravine. Mario managed to have the children on his side, an expert at playing the victim and better yet, manipulating and twisting situations in his favour; he managed to make his children prefer to stay and live with him and not with her. During that time, Esmeralda felt as if the world were collapsing, that she was dying and going mad with grief, frustration and helplessness in the face of such a painful decision that her children had made. She couldn't believe it, she couldn't accept what she had just heard when he asked each of them, sitting with his children on Victoria's bed and hugging them, while Esmeralda was in front, standing in the doorway, having just arrived after hearing Mario calling her because they had something very important to talk about. To this day, Esmeralda is haunted by that image like a never ending nightmare, she vividly remembers the image of her three children sitting next to her ex-husband as if he were protecting them from her and, what he had asked them and their answer echoes in her ears and resounds in her head as if it were going to explode. Speaking in a victimized voice, he began with Apollo:

–My son, who do you want to live with, your mum or me? –he asked each and every one of them and, one by one they answered:

–With you, daddy, not with mummy.

It was the worst, most cruel and painful situation that she had ever lived in her entire life, a fact that she never imagined could have happened to her, she had never thought about it, it had never crossed her mind, she had never expected to feel rejected by her own children whom she had practically raised all on her own, while their father had dedicated himself to living the high life, making the nights days and sharing with his mistresses; jealous and treating Esmeralda inhumanely, controlling her life, limiting and forbidding her everything, it bothered him greatly that she worked, he demanded and controlled the time she left and returned home, she couldn't be a minute late and, he never allowed her to do a training course or attend a work meeting outside the city, because the thought of Esmeralda sleeping somewhere else generated uncontrollable jealousy in him, he would go mad, become irritable and aggressive, treating her as if she were a bad woman and even hitting her.

Esmeralda lived with bruises all over her body, although not on her face, and she suffered from repeated gynaecologist diseases as a result of Mario's infidelities. It was very unfortunate for her that the children grew closer to their father than to her, he had great facility to express his feelings and affection, the good and bad, becoming an extremist in his reactions. He could be very sweet, playful and easy to get along, as well as easily explode for insignificant situations, reacting like a true demon, expelling flames with his hurtful words, destroying everything and reaching humiliating situations like spitting in her face. However, he had always been more expressive and affectionate than Esmeralda; he came from a family that was used to expressing their feelings of affection with hugs, caresses and beautiful words, as well as with screams. On the other hand, Esmeralda had been born and raised in the countryside; they were six siblings and, her mother and father came from even larger families, of twelve and fourteen children, families in which food was the way to express love and concern. The more chunky, chubby and rosy cheeked they looked, it was a sign of being healthy and above all, it was a sign of being the children of good parents, regardless of whether they were caressed, hugged or cuddled. That's the way most families who lived in the countryside were, where working the land and raising animals was the centre of everything. Her mother would get up at dawn to milk the cows before preparing breakfast and sending the children to school, and then dedicated herself to making lunch for dozens of workers, because in those years it was common to make lunch for the workers, in addition to cooking with firewood, making homemade traditional Chilean bread, hand-washing clothes and taking care and feeding the animals such as chickens, ducks, turkeys, lambs, pigs and cows. It is very difficult for Esmeralda to imagine how her mother managed to do so many things.

Despite the great work that was done in the fields, Esmeralda had memories of a happy childhood, where all her family members were involved in the field work. The children from a very young age assumed responsibilities that seemed like a game to them, such as for example, helping to irrigate the crops: the children would sit at the end of the corn or bean rows, or whatever it was, while their father or a worker was at the beginning of the row, opening and closing blocks, letting the water drain to hydrate the crops; the children had to wait for the water to reach the other end and let them know of this so that they could move on to the next row. Esmeralda remembered with great emotion when she collected chicken and duck eggs, being a great joy when she would find in a fence's blackberries and under an old and disused machinery, a nest full of eggs; she would roll up her dress to serve as a basket and would collect them and take them to her mother, who would get very happy because she had prevented the dogs from eating them. She also remembered cutting green beans, shucking corn, going with her father fishing in the river, releasing and enclosing the animals, feeding them and even cleaning the pig pen; that was life in the countryside, there was no time for hugs or cuddles, but she was a happy girl, feeling loved and protected. She didn't remember her father or mother hugging or showing them affection, but she didn't miss it either because they had never received it.

Esmeralda became aware of the forms of physical expression of affection between parents and children while in university, when she saw the way, her classmates related to their parents and friends and, what seemed almost impossible for her to do, even to this day, was the fact that she couldn't hug and show affection to her parents or siblings and, none of them could do it to each other. They greet with a hello and at most with a kiss on the cheek, whenever they see each other again after several months and even years. Despite wanting and trying to be more affectionate, she couldn't, something would stop her as she attempted it, shaking her father's hand and kissing her mother on the cheek. On the contrary, she was extremely loving with her friends, affectionate and even sometimes euphoric with her greetings, hugs and kisses and, with ease, she could express her feelings, being very natural and spontaneous when saying to a girl or boy friend, "I love you", "I miss you", "I love the way you are", "Wow, you're really outgoing"," You are important to me"," I thank you from the bottom of my heart, I'm privileged and very proud that we are friends", and phrases like that.

With her children, ever since they were born, she had been very loving and concerned about their upbringing and education, although also very severe and demanding, punishing and setting ground rules, discipline and habits. On the contrary, Mario was very expressive, loving, generous and spoiled them and, when it came to a "no", for example, "you don't have permission to go to the party or stay overnight at your friend's house", he would tell them:

–Ask your mother, she knows whether or not to give you permission.

And that's how he always faced complex situations and set boundaries. On the other hand, living a life of domestic violence, with a husband of an explosive, dominant, misogynist and abusive character, made her a very sad, nervous, emotional and short-tempered woman, reacting many times inappropriately with her children, yelling at them and not being so loving and affectionate. He, on his part, was very playful and mischievous, he made them laugh a lot, although he was still very severe and yelled at them with insults and treated them in a very aggressive way, but the children learned and got used to living among a mixture of love and fear of their father, while their mother was more about nurturing and controlling.

However, the lack of physical and verbal expression of affection, even if it's true that she didn't need it, didn't help her in any way when it came to expressing her own feelings and experiencing love, cherishing her children and being very affectionate towards them; she wasn't as expressive as Mario, besides that, as a mother, she had the role of instilling habits, routines and good teachings, while their father was dedicated to playing, entertaining and spoiling them, often undermining Esmeralda:

–Don't listen to that old lady, your mother is crazy.

Other wonderful memories of Esmeralda's childhood were the summer school holidays, which began before Christmas and ended the last days of February. They were summers of great joy, fun, games and adventures when her cousins would arrive from Santiago, spending the entire summer holidays season in the countryside, playing every day and night, swimming in the river and lagoon, playing circus, hide and seek, ball, and cutting blackberries so her aunt Carmencita could make jams; she was very affectionate, tender and sweet, she would bring them many gifts and sweets, she was very loved and everyone's favourite aunt. The children were very helpful during the harvest and they loved being a part of the chicha (corn beer) making process, cutting watermelons and melons and, riding carts, threshing and plough machines. The nights were long awaited, everyone sitting around a pile of corn shucking one by one, waiting for it to get dark; time flew by and, they laughed at the stories and jokes that were told. There were also scary nights, in which fear paralyzed them when they heard stories and legends of the devil, ghosts and shrines built in public spaces as a reminder of tragic deaths, along with the stories of goblins and *la llorona,* a legend that exists in almost all countries of Latin America about the ghost of a woman who roams waterfront areas mourning her children that drowned. Her incursion into the world of mining kept her highly motivated with work, as did her postgraduate studies; both challenges demanded a lot of work, study and time. Thanks to her great communication, public relations and negotiation skills, it was easy for her to access the headship and nail down important volumes of sales; meanwhile, her experience and professional training as a social worker, added to her joviality, sympathy, spontaneity, intelligence and tendency to make jokes and mischief. This allowed her to have an excellent connection with the workers, making very pleasant educational seminars, with audiences that could be of just one person, one to one, or small groups of fifteen or twenty workers and up to one hundred people and, her biggest record was an audience of six hundred workers, at seven in the morning, on the beach, in front of the ocean, an educational job she had done for a transnational company responsible for the construction project of an ocean water desalination plant, to supply drinking water to a large American mining company; that was an incredible experience. She had been contacted by Gunther, the professional expert in risk prevention and in charge of the security of said company, who had asked her to carry out educational work for the employees of his company, as an after-sales service. Since she was an excellent client due to the large volume of purchases of Sunnywork sunscreen, she agreed, but under certain conditions, such as accommodation and food. With more than a year working and her experience in the mining world, she had learned to negotiate and request certain minimum facilities to carry out her educational work in a more professional and comfortable way, for the workers and for herself. It made her insecure and she avoided driving under the thick morning *camanchaca* cloud, a dense fog in the Chilean coast, like in old England, climatic conditions that made visibility difficult, increasing the risks of car accidents. That afternoon when she arrived at the port of Caldera, Gunther joined her for dinner and then took her to see the place where she would carry out her educational work. She was pleasantly surprised; smiling and flirtatious, he said while showing her the place where the activities would be held:

–Look, I had a stage built especially for you, it's a platform where you'll be two meters higher than sea level and the workers will be able to see you from everywhere.

–Wow, you've outdone yourself! Thank you very much for the great consideration and detail!

She was very happy, although the place was as big as a soccer stadium. In short, she had to carry on with the job. The next day he picked her up at the cabin at six o'clock in the morning so she would go with him to the headship meeting, because once that important meeting was finished where they announced the guidelines for the day's work, his intervention in the field came right after, not giving him enough time to later pick her up.

When they arrived at the meeting lounge, there were approximately thirty people, all men, headships of different areas. Gunther approached the manager and informed him that he was accompanied by the professional representative of Sunnywork's pharmaceutical chemical laboratory, who would be carrying out the educational work for the employees; and this one didn't object to Esmeralda's presence at the meeting.

She felt observed, he was a foreign-looking man, American to be more precise, who stared at her, with very bright eyes and a soft smile, making the situation a bit uncomfortable; however, as he seemed to be quite an older person, she tried to ignore it –in addition to the fact that she was used to being looked at in a mischievous and flirtatious way, being frequently complimented and told a series of flattering phrases, even though there were some who crossed the line at times, having someone always in charge of putting them in their place, caring for and protecting Esmeralda and the company's prestige–, she concentrated on paying attention to the meeting. The person who was in charge gave the floor to the man who wouldn't take his eyes off her, who responded in a very relaxed and smiling tone, with an excellent command of Spanish and with an American accent:

–Don't worry, carry on with the meeting, today I will be a spectator, as well as the beautiful young lady who accompanies us and who will give the induction speech; I'm sure it will be very interesting and a great honour to listen to her speak, he said, smiling and still looking at her while everyone smiled approvingly also staring at her. Esmeralda was curious to know who the man was and asked Gunther, who replied that he was the big boss, the representative of the transnational in Chile, adding in a jokingly and smiling tone:

–He's American; with him, you can practice and keep learning how to speak English.

After the meeting, they all went outside to the area where Esmeralda had to give the seminar, her being shocked to see the large number of workers, all standing, completely covering the area that she had called a soccer stadium. There were about six hundred workers, all of them wearing overalls and safety jackets, the bright orange colour and different coloured helmets standing out, which differentiated the area and the company in which they worked. Everyone looked expectant and Esmeralda was terrified. She tried to keep herself composed, professional and firm. The two security guards accompanied her to the podium, greeted the workers and asked them to be quiet so they could listen to the young lady who was going to give them the seminar on how to use the sunscreen.

Esmeralda had to shout to be heard and, as she talked, she gained more confidence and empowerment in her educational role, she did it in an agile and dynamic way, entertaining, making jokes, being her typical self that always gave her very good results.

A Sunscreen seminar

For the demonstration of the correct application and use of the sunscreen, she requested the support of two volunteers, who were very happy to have the young lady apply sunscreen on their faces, when they saw how she placed a small amount on her hand and then delicately applied it on her face, avoiding the eye area due to the strong irritation it caused; once the application was finished, she asked in a very friendly way:

–Which one of you wants to be my first volunteer? –There was always one; the one that believed himself to be the young man in the movie, the matador, the one who carries it. Esmeralda began by asking him if he applied sunscreen or not, how many times a day, if he had any complications or bad reactions.

And meanwhile his co-workers made jokes, like for example:

–Dude, I didn't think you were that manly to volunteer, tell the young lady that your boyfriend applies your sunscreen, –causing everyone to laugh.

However, she had the best joke:

–OK Juanito, are you ready for the demonstration to begin?

–Yes, ma'am, I'm ready, go ahead and apply Sunnywork on my face –as he extended his neck and tilted his head to the side stretching his skin.

His co-workers continued to make jokes and many of them regretted not volunteering. At that moment, Esmeralda did her thing:

–So, are you ready for the application of Sunnywork on your face?

–Yes, I'm ready, ma'am, go ahead and apply the sunscreen on me – tilting his cheek even more and wiping off any dust he could have had.

–OK Juanito, give me your hand so I can put the right amount...

She didn't manage to finish the sentence when her volunteer was left shamefaced and everyone making fun and laughing at him out loud, even the experts in risk prevention who accompanied Esmeralda and herself couldn't stop laughing.

Esmeralda felt like Marilyn Monroe on the podium with the hundreds of workers applauding and cheering her on, some even shouting "idol"!, while most laughed and made fun of their co-worker, who had gone for the gold and had left with coal and in front of all of them. Esmeralda was used to making jokes, it was her way of getting through things, doing it very cunningly and fun; being mischievous also helped her to easily overcome situations that could have been complex, as well as to break the ice.

Esmeralda was feeling like Marilyn Monroe

After the meeting and once the induction seminar was over, Gunther introduced her to the big boss, who shook her hand while congratulating and thanking her for the excellent seminar, telling her that he had been impressed by her ability to handle herself on stage, her confidence and professionalism with which she had addressed so many workers. Esmeralda thanked him with a smile. His name was William and, he gifted her with a pen-drive saying:

–I'm giving you this pen-drive as a gift with some of my favourite songs, I write the lyrics of my songs and I also play the music for other artists with my guitar.

–Ah, thank you very much, you are so kind.

–I would like you to listen and get your feedback on them.

From that day on and for the span of a month, every afternoon and evening he delighted her with his music, romantic, very sweet, even church songs, which he interpreted to the rhythm of his guitar over the phone, yes, every afternoon he would send her on cloud nine with the gift of his sweetness, dedication and music, forming a beautiful friendship between them. He managed to take her to the different sites of his company so he could see her, inviting her to share exquisite lunches.

Esmeralda felt very loved and spoiled; she saw William as a very special man, and yes, he was, everyone respected and loved him dearly and not because he was the big boss, he was admired for radiating peace and love, possessing an extraordinary sympathy and humility, with boundless generosity. She felt great love for him, he was a mixture of father and priest, who spoiled her and with whom she felt safe, finding calmness and peace. They enjoyed exquisite lunches on the beachfront, making their mouths water when they remembered and imagined a steaming pan of garlic shrimp and grilled tilapia with hearts of palm and avocado, what a delight! In front of the ocean in Bahía Inglesa, sitting on the terrace of the famous El Platea'o Resto Bar and in the restaurant of the Rocas de Bahía Hotel, likewise when he invited her to lunch at the restaurant El Mira Mar de Caldera, owned by his friend Rigo Ibarra and Cecilia, she loved to serve herself those freshly baked bread rolls with garlic and coriander butter, waiting for the *locos con salsa verde* (molluscs with green sauce) that were another delight. William spoiled her a lot, and even tried to incorporate her into his company. She remembers that he was a casino fan; he spent nights playing at the slot machines, in fact, most of the weekends he travelled from Bahía Inglesa to Copiapó and stayed at the Antay Casino and Hotel Copiapó just to relax and enjoy playing. She joined him every time, he would tell her that she brought him good luck, and in fact he almost always won a lot of money with the games she made, exclaiming with great joy and wisdom:

–You win because you don't play out of ambition; with your innocence you attract money because you don't covet it.

In fact, Esmeralda only played for fun; she loved listening to the music of the slot machines, she'd go crazy when she'd win because of the noise the coins made as they dropped and the sound of winners' music, it was like a carnival and fireworks.

Esmeralda couldn't stand having to wear her field work clothes and, in particular safety shoes and boots bothered her greatly, they were really uncomfortable, made her feel trapped, suffocated and, even more so during the summer when the heat was unbearable and she had to wear boots, jeans, a jacket, helmet, glasses and even ear protectors; as there were some gentlemen with whom she had to interact who were extremely rigorous with the protocols and; wouldn't allow her not to use one hundred per cent of the safety equipment. One of them was the famous Pablo Sánchez, who was very strange, hallucinating that he came from planet Jupiter; he was such a rare specimen, those ones who you encounter sometimes in life, even on his Facebook page he identified himself as: pabloJupiterpoorHouseCatwithAIDS ... who can identify himself with that name? only Pablo, anyway, he also had his human traits and streaks of sensitivity.

One day, when touring the different areas of the project inside the *Caserones* site, Pablo warned her that they were going to cross a small path with water as a result of melted snow from the mountain range; Esmeralda, seeing the crystal clear water and the reflection of the pebbles of different shades of brown that stood out with the sun's rays, begged like a little girl, with her hands together in front of her face in a prayer position:

–Please, please, can we stop to touch the water?

Pablo frowned at her as he stopped the truck. Esmeralda opened the door and without getting out, enjoyed playing with the water and pulling out handfuls of pebbles. As they continued on their way to do another educational seminar, Pablo looked at her sarcastically and commented in a questioning tone:

–If you want, I can take you where there's snow, in case you want to play again.

–Yes, yes, please, and you can take pictures of me –she responded euphoric, very happy and impatient.

–So, you can send them to your boss? –he added in a serious tone, both bursting into a contagious laughter. And just like that, a more personable relationship was built and magically increasing Sunnywork's purchase orders.

She truly enjoyed that day, she always enjoyed everything she did, being happy with very little, with simple things and in contact with nature. Ending the day with something that was of maximum freedom and joy, as soon as she crossed the security barrier to exit the *Caserones* mining site, she stopped the car, remaining seated behind the wheel, took off one of her boots and strongly threw it in the back, and then doing the same with the other; she lowered the windows, put the speakers on blast and went down from the top of the hill singing, her hair blowing with the wind and trying to catch the air with her hand, she loved feeling that exquisite sensation of the force of the wind on her hand, it reminded her of all the times she had gone tandem jumping and skydiving.

After visiting her daughter Victoria and spoiling her little grandson, she went home to do the administrative work that was very tedious, because she had to record even the smallest detail carried out during the day, including the beginning and end time of each interview and educational work, considering where, with whom, how many, objective, results, impacts, too much, too much! It was already close to eleven o'clock at night, her body was giving out and she fell exhausted into Morpheus's arms. At midnight she was awakened by a phone call, half asleep and awake she answered thinking that it could be an emergency, but no, it was her friend Alejandrina:

–Esmeralda, Esmeralda, my friend, let's go to the nightclub – inviting her with extreme excitement, to which half asleep she replied:

–No, I can't, thank you though, but I'm extremely exhausted.

–What? Don't tell me you're in bed, you, the Sunnywork girl, on a Friday night?

–I'm exhausted, my friend, let me sleep.

–Get up, woman, the night is life and there's only one life.

She managed to convince her to get up, and indeed they had a great time talking, sharing a snack, drinking and dancing.

Her friend Alejandrina was a very important part of her life, united by their profession, challenges, family events, a life of push and pull and, above all, a lot of fun and adventures. On weekends they would hang out at pubs and nightclubs, they loved to dance until the club closed at around five or six in the morning. Alejandrina had a very strong personality and made things very clear from the beginning. One of the first times they went out at night, she looked into her eyes in a determined and dictatorial way, implanting one of her rules:

–We are going out together, but independently.

–How's that?

–Each one in their own car.

–But how if we live so close and, sometimes it's so hard to find a parking space?

–That's not my problem; you'll manage to find a parking space.

–Are you crazy, my friend, what did you eat today or what bit you?

–What happens, Esmeralda, is that, if one of us wants to leave early because we're tired, sleepy or simply just want to go home and, the other is having a great time and doesn't want to go home, it's simple, she gets in her car and goes home; why make the other one go home as well if she's having a blast and maybe perhaps could be her lucky night. No, my friend, we have to be grown women, don't you think?

–Alright, yeah, you're right. Oh, that's a great song.

–See, OK get ready and let's go dancing, because I love that song too.

Little by little, she shook off the prejudices and obstacles that had prevented her from being fully happy, empowering herself and enjoying her freedom as a happily divorced woman, without the intention of getting into a new relationship or falling in love and, even less remarrying. Being in a relationship wasn't in her plans, she definitely didn't see it necessary to have a new lover, the experience she had had with the father of her children, had been enough and more. She was enjoying herself and had everything to be happy, except for a better bond with her children.

Her friends forever Ilse, Alejandrina, Marcelita and Silvana

When they inaugurated the Antay Casino of Copiapó, it was a huge event at regional level. The project had some adversaries but the pro casino predominated, giving the city of Copiapó a new air, responding to a series of needs and services for its inhabitants, tourists and businessmen and even for the government, which meant a true cultural rebirth, with events and fun, a gigantic project that included a five-star hotel, swimming pools, cinemas, event and meeting venues, restaurants and bars. For the opening of the Antay casino and nightclub, they sent her a VIP invitation, which consisted of a free entrance to that casino and nightclub, being able to bring up to seven friends, who could make use of the same privileges as Esmeralda, which meant free entry and a complimentary drink. She enjoyed herself to the fullest from Thursday to Saturday, three days in a row dancing until dawn; she became very popular surrounded by many friends, from her university where she was studying her Masters and acquaintances from work, in short, friends flourished like the flowers in the Atacama Desert after a copious rain. In Esmeralda's case, it was because of her joviality and facility to make friends, besides the free access to the nightclub. There were days when she would come home exhausted after a hard day at work, at times having to get up at dawn, driving two or three hours to get to certain mining site to give the induction speech at seven in the morning before the staff began their work day. Despite being very exhausted, lying down and even sleeping, many times she would wake up after the insistent and irresistible calls from her friends, who managed to convince her to get up, take another good cold shower, have a couple of energy drinks with Coca-Cola and completely wake up refreshed and animated. Her friends would applaud when she'd arrived and when dancing like crazy, singing and enjoying the night, making jokes about her:

–Look everyone, isn't that the sleeping beauty?

–She didn't want to get up and look at how she's dancing; she looks like the queen of the dance floor.

–You mean queen of the night?

With the versatility that characterized her and her facility of adapting to different situations, she always did what came to mind; no matter how far-fetched and childish it seemed to others, she simply did it without even thinking twice about it. What she was always aware of, was to never harm another person.

In her little white dove, she always kept several changes of clothes, from her work clothes and the typical jacket, gloves and hat to keep warm to formal clothes for an interview with some manager of supplies and acquisitions, visits to the doctors or pharmacy; being essential a casual outfit to go to the pub or the casino, when it became late on her way back from work. The most important thing that she loved was always having on hand bathing suit and beach clothes; it was wonderful to arrive at Bahía Inglesa at six or seven in the afternoon, take off her miner clothes, put on her bathing suit and run to dive in the water, laughing alone remembering how in Montego Bay she'd do the same, trying to avoid the lifeguards from seeing her.

That is how one day, coming down from the Manto Verde Company, it occurred to her to surprise her friend Cecilia Díaz, the midwife, who always commented that she was spending a fabulous holiday in Villa Alegre, a small beach near Chañaral. When she arrived and saw the beauty of the place, she was stunned. The family home she owned, she had inherited from her father who had worked all his life in the national railway company, having the great opportunity to acquire that wonderful summer house with a more than privileged location; with soft golden sands, crystal clear waters with almost no waves, which was the continuation of the terrace, enjoying a spectacular afternoon with her friend Cecilia, swimming, sunbathing and "talking about the human and the divine", as she would always say. It was an excellent way to end her workday, returning home at night, very happy to rest.

One day, her daughter Victoria came to drop off the baby because she was going out; she played a lot with her little grandson who was allowed to do whatever he wanted so then he could quickly fall asleep. However, she had to sleep with one eye open, as they would say in the countryside, making sure that her little grandson Viccencito didn't fall out of bed or fell asleep uncovered. The next day, he would wake her up very early asking for milk; she would quickly prepare the bottle, take a shower, have breakfast, and leave him at his mother's house, continuing her way in a rush to the university, since classes were during the daytime and on Saturdays.

Among the new friends she made working at the mine, was Marsella, a sales executive and representative of one of the distribution companies of her star product, Sunnywork, and Karlita Hernández, who worked in the area of safety and risk prevention, with whom she often got together to plan field routes, visiting the same companies and clients, boosting sales and follow-up services, making the field trips very short and entertaining. One day, at lunchtime, the sun was beginning to feel strong, hot summer sun, after finishing a few meetings and interviews at fishing companies and the project of the water desalination plant in the port of Caldera, they decided to go to lunch on the beach; together with her friends and co-workers, Erika, Maritza and Kahina, they dressed as they were supposed to and following the protocol for field work, safety clothing, including helmets and boots. Looking like that, they decided to take a couple of pictures on the beach before having lunch, posing on the waterfront of Bahía Inglesa with the ocean behind them. They would take pictures with their helmets on and off, laughing a lot, until Esmeralda came up with the brilliant idea of taking a picture throwing their helmets in the air, just like in the American movies, where the students throw their caps in the air once the graduation ceremony is over, turning out to be a very fun and, immortalizing the image in a very festive and peculiar picture.

Throwing the mining helmets in the air

Karlita, Esmeralda, Kahina, Marsella and Maritza

William wouldn't give up, with patience and seductive perseverance in the conquest of his beloved and dreamed Esmeralda, pleasing her to the fullest. It was the end of the year and Christmas was just around the corner; for Esmeralda it was a date of deep pain and anguish that began to invade her thoughts, being prey to an overwhelming sadness and frustration because it meant that she wouldn't be able to share with her children and beloved grandson since Victoria would surely choose to enjoy Christmas dinner with her father. This made Esmeralda's presence practically impossible, due to the tension that was generated as a result of the inappropriate way that her ex-husband referred to her, with irony and sarcasm, causing a very uncomfortable atmosphere for the whole family. For this reason, she preferred not to spend important dates together such as Christmas, New Years and birthdays, but instead taking turns each year; although he never respected the agreements and Esmeralda always ended up alone, with all the preparations made and a mother's broken dreams, submerged in a sea of tears, despair and anguish, a crisis difficult to recover from due to the emotional fragility she was in because of her severe depression, having attempted to end her life on multiple occasions.

On Christmas Eve, Esmeralda was in the garden playing with her dog Lady's puppies, being surprised when she heard her name from the fence in the front garden; the voice sounded familiar, but she couldn't recognize it, she couldn't react until she opened the door and found William on a brand new bicycle adorned with a huge bow on the basket as a symbol of a gift. With a wide smile and very happy, he got off the bike saying:

–Look! Do you like it? It's for you; it's your Christmas present.

Esmeralda placed her hand on her face jumping of joy, and exclaimed:

–Wow, I can't believe it! Yes, yes, I love it, thank you very much, you've really outdone yourself!

He handed it over to her, leaving immediately and almost running, he had come in the company car and was accompanied by a couple of workers, who were in a hurry to get back to their homes.

The beautiful bicycle

Esmeralda, despite wearing a formal dress and heels, couldn't resist the urge to take a ride on her beautiful bike and, as she could, she got on and took it for a spin around the block; but the return was difficult because her house was located at the top of the hill. The neighbours looked at her with approval and her neighbour Elsita commented:

–You can tell that the American is in love with you, Esmeralda. Why don't you accept him as your boyfriend? You are very beautiful and live alone, you need and deserve the good company of a man, and who better than him, you can tell that he really loves you, just look, he spoils you like a little girl.

Indeed, William was a very thoughtful and generous man, a real gentleman; he knew how to make people happy, like the great surprise he had given her by buying the beautiful aqua green bicycle that had captured his attention at the mall. That night on the way to dinner, enthralled like a child, she approached the bicycle, touched it as if she were caressing it, gazing at the wonderful basket it had on the back, which made the bike have a more feminine and even flirtatious look. She imagined the basket filled with daisies, wild flowers that she would cut by the shore of a small stream, or from a lake and in the middle of a field. She spent only a few seconds appreciating the beauty of the bike, without making any comments and, then continued walking towards the restaurant.

A couple of days later, having dinner, he told her that he would be travelling to California to spend the end of the year holidays, taking three weeks off and that it would mean the world if she would go with him. Esmeralda, with pain in her heart, refused the invitation to avoid generating false expectations in him, she saw him as a father, as a great friend whom she could trust, feel safe, be herself without any restriction or self-protection; she couldn't see him as a man. Instead, he saw her as a woman, he was totally in love with her, to the point that he wrote her a wonderful love song, saying that he had fallen in love with her as soon as she had entered the office where they were meeting, that she took his breath away and he couldn't continue leading the meeting.

"So in Love" https://bit.ly/2QuhPvb

He strangely commented that, he didn't understand how she wasn't interested in marrying, since all the single and divorced women he knew, the only thing they longed for was to get married and, that they walked around with the dress in their handbags. But that was definitely not the case of Esmeralda, she was very happy being free as a divorced woman, a second relationship was not in her plans and even less remarrying.

The Christmas before her trip to London was destined to be spent completely alone. She could have accepted the dinner invitation at her closest friend's house, but no, it was inappropriate and it would have been tremendously devastating seeing all the love and expressions of affection from family members wherever she would have been; thinking of how sad and devastating it was not being able to share with her children on such a momentous date of love and family union, she would have felt despised, abandoned and would have tried to distract her mind by staying busy.

In moments of anxiety, crises and anguish, that had accentuated during and after Christmas time, and after her trip to London, she resorted to emergency therapy where her psychologist friend Alberto would make her react and abruptly wake up with shock therapies; in a strong and dominant voice he would say:

–React, woman, how dare you cry while they are having a great time? Tell me, does crying, feeling sorry for yourself and wanting to commit suicide help you, no, right? Stop trying to play a happy family, that's over and it has been for a while –and he would change the subject—, now, tell me, how was England, why didn't you stay there, what did you come here to do, if you say that nobody here loves you.

At the end, they would end up laughing like great friends.

When they were calm, he took the opportunity to ask her about her experiences in England; she told him about her friend Terry, to which Alberto exclaimed with joy:

–Ah, you were keeping that a secret, so you had a lover during your stay in England and you didn't want to tell me about it.

–No, no, it's not a big deal; let me tell you about it: I had signed up on a blind dating website where I met Terry.

And he replied very interested:

–Oh, that's interesting, tell me about it, do those Internet encounters work out?

–I don't know, we became friends and went out five times – yes, she was very sure of that, they had gone out only five times, making it very clear that they weren't in a relationship and, continued saying:

–We went out during my last month in London, before returning to Chile, he liked me, but I wasn't interested in him, you know, I don't want a serious relationship with anyone.

–And why not? Who forbids it? You're a young lady and very good looking.

–Stop with the nonsense, the thing is that, since I didn't want anything with him nor anyone, when he would pick me up or we agreed on going out, I would wear my worst clothes, wouldn't put makeup on and would try to look the most unkempt and ugliest possible...

Alberto interrupted, chuckling, leaving her stunned without understanding what had caused him so much amusement and, she looked at him with a questioning face, raising her shoulders and spreading her arms out with her palms up in search of an explanation:

–Ay, woman, you are one of a kind!

–What's so special about me, why do you say I'm one of a kind, and why are you laughing so much?

–It's just that you're so pretty Esmeralda, you caused the opposite effect on him.-Women are erroneously used to, in order to look beautiful, to wear the most eye-catching outfits they have and even with glitter, they exaggerate their makeup making them look fake, they can seem pretty, it's true, however, not attractive because it's an artificial beauty, hiding their natural appearance under so much clothing, glitter and kilos of makeup. On the other hand, you did the exact opposite by wanting to show yourself unattractive, ugly, go under the radar and even messy so that he wouldn't notice you and lose his interest and, what happened? Among all the ugly and the matchless clothes and no makeup –he exclaimed, raising his voice and arms– you caused the opposite effect! It highlighted your natural beauty, by not wearing makeup your face's beautiful natural features stood out and shined, showing the transparency and brightness of your eyes, with that naive and angelic appearance that you have, that's what happened, the only thing that was missing was you not bathing so that that you would smell bad.

He kindly laughed, causing her to inevitably join in:

–No, no, I didn't get that far, I bathed every day, ah, but ate a lot of raw garlic so my breath would smell and drive him kilometres away and avoid him from trying to kiss me, haha!

–Really? No, really...no, I don't believe you...

–Obviously not, it was a joke.

–Come on, girl, you're healthier than a lettuce.

Sharing with her grandson Viccencito was her greatest pleasure and blessing, who used to spend Friday or Saturday nights with her, while his parents went out to a party and, on the next day it would be her turn to go out, taking turns with Victoria, although her daughter would always protest when Esmeralda wasn't able to take care of her grandson because she had already made plans to go out with her friends, to which Victoria angrily would reply:

–I'm young and have the right to go out, not you, you're an old woman, a grandmother, you have to stay home, you're making a fool out of yourself by going out dancing at nightclubs; I hope to God I don't run into you; I'd die of embarrassment.

That was the usual way Victoria referred to her mother, in a very hurtful and cruel way and, she had learned it from her father. Unfortunately, Esmeralda had to put up with the insults, if she answered back, she would get angry and insult her as if she were her enemy. Worse still, she would manipulate her by denying her from seeing her little grandson. Given this circumstance, Esmeralda kept quiet in order to avoid further discussions and to be able to see and share with her adorable little grandson.

Esmeralda enjoyed as much or even more the company of her grandson, she spoiled him and played with him whenever she had the chance, she loved to empower him, make him feel that he had super powers and treat him like a big boy, for example, she would say to him:

–Vicci, can you come with me to put gasoline in my car?

He would smile even with his eyes and run up to get on the white dove; he would happily go because he knew and loved that his grandmother allowed him to pump the car with gasoline, holding the hose while the tank filled up and, he would ask with a tenderness that melted her with love:

–Grandma Esmeralda, why do you let me pour gasoline into your car and my dad won't?

Smilingly she would reply:

–Because I have patience and love to make you happy, I love you.

Every moment lived with her little grandson Viccencito was sublime

Ah! And going to the mall was the best for him at two years old; before reaching the main entrance of the mall, she would check that no one was coming near that could possibly ruin her plan, and would say:

–Viccencito, did you know that if you tell the door to open, it will open so we can pass through?

And he would look at her in disbelief, but wanting to try, with his little eyes wide open, pumping his chest, raising a hand and with a commanding voice, would repeat what his grandmother had told him to say:

–Door, open, I'm coming through –and the immense glass doors would magically open before his eyes and when passing the doorway, he would say the second command:

–Doors, close! –thus magically closing them.

And that's how they began their entry to the mall to buy something delicious to share. Another magic trick was crossing the streets, also through super-power games, which empowered him and generated feelings of security by allowing him to form a confident personality and high self-esteem. Before crossing the street, in the pedestrian crossing and at the precise moment the traffic light changed, he would stretch his little hand out, while crossing saying to the drivers:

–Stop, stop, I'm crossing the street.

Visits to the fire station, where his grandmother was a volunteer, were of maximum fascination for Viccencito; riding on the trucks was a great adventure and, a little more daring and yet fun one, was dancing while the truck gently swerved from side to side to the rhythm of the music.

Sharing with her grandson Viccencito

was her greatest pleasure and blessing

Caldera, III Region Atacama Chile

CHAPTER IV

Avoiding a new relationship

The trip that Terry made from London to Chile, expressly and exclusively to visit Esmeralda, arose from her way of being, so naive and spontaneous, who was fascinated with the phenomenon of the flowery Atacama Desert, which was in its maximum splendour and peak, covering plains and hills with beautiful and varied species of flowers that looked like real colourful carpets, where a wonderful fuchsia colour predominated, bringing back the memory of the image of freshly peeled beets and her grandmother Safira's velvet armchairs; likewise, majestic landscapes of lush and gleaming red and yellow Rhodophiala flowers, flora and fauna that made the most arid desert in the world completely disappear, at least for about three months. A lover of nature and the desert, she had visited it several times with her friends and had even taken Fernando Del Pozo, her Economics and Globalization professor, who had travelled expressly from Madrid, Spain, on behalf of a prestigious Madrid university, to teach classes in the Master's in Business

Administration that she was studying. She took the most extraordinary and unique walks and excursions with her dear friend Nelson, united by his love for nature, the desert and Celtic music and with; whom she would go on excursions on Sundays. He would pick her up very early to seize the day, walking through the desert on inhospitable but amazing paths and trails in the eyes of an excursionist. Their trips to the flowery desert began with the awakening of the first wild flowers, going through the emotion of appreciating the beauty of the first Rhodophialas, visiting remote places in search of extraordinary species such as the lion's claw and the fox's ears, plants native to Chile.

Opportunities in which they would take countless photographs, Esmeralda posting on Facebook one of the beautiful photos in which she was posing in the middle, tagging fifty friends from all over the world, whom she had met during her six months in London and during the trips she had taken with her magical little red shoes.

She invited them to visit and enjoy the flowery Atacama Desert, a unique phenomenon in the world, offering them to stay at her home. That is how a large majority of her friends responded amazed and admired with such natural beauty and, at the same time, regretting not being able to travel, while receiving three comments from those who did wish to travel: her friend Elena Aguilera from Catalonia, Luzia from Brazil and Terry from London.

The photograph that would make a 180 degree

turn in Esmeralda's life

Esmeralda, with the same naturalness with which she invited them, replied: "excellent, I'm glad to know that you all wish to come". After three days, she received an email from Terry, reiterating his gratitude for such a warm and generous invitation and, letting her know that he would be arriving in two weeks, attaching a file with the tickets and asking questions about some details of the trip, like if he needed to get any vaccination or carry some type of repellent to avoid being bitten by mosquitoes, and so on. Stunned, she couldn't believe what she was reading, as she shook her head energetically from side to side and with her eyes fixed on the email, saying to herself:

–No, no, this can't be, this can't be happening to me –she abruptly stood up and began to walk back and forth in her house out of desperation, sweating and feeling a panic and anxiety attack, thinking aloud:

–This man is crazy, how can he think that he is going to come to my house, doesn't he understand that when someone says I'm going to go to your house or they tell you come and see me, you never go, it's just a figure of speech.

In that reaction, she stopped walking and, placing her hands on her temples, exclaimed:

–English fool! That's the problem. The English take everything so literal.

Calmer and understanding what had happened, she began to look for the best strategy to answer the email, letting him know that he wasn't going to travel, that it had been a misunderstanding, that she couldn't receive him in her home. She was going crazy, the sweat and the difficulties to breathe, brought to mind the image of the last time she had seen him; it had been at the Embankment Station, desperately leaving to avoid being kissed and, now he wanted to stay at her house, no, no, that couldn't be. She turned off the computer, got in her car and drove off without a destination. Her friends were laughing nonstop with what Esmeralda was going through, making many jokes about it:

–Luckily not everyone said they'd come to see the flowery desert; how would you accommodate them all?

–Only you could think of inviting the whole world.

–The English are fools with goggles, they walk in a straight line and go directly where they are told or invited.

Her guy friends became jealous:

–I, your friend, the handkerchief to your tears, haven't even been invited to your house for a cup of coffee and, you plan on receiving a UK man for three weeks? You are so inconsiderate with our friendship; I can't forgive that.

–But I didn't invite him nor do I want him to come.

–And what are you going to do? Or do you plan on telling him not to travel?

–Exactly, that's what I'm going to reply, for him not to travel.

–You can't do that, it's not his fault, it's your error and you must face it.

–But how, can he sleep at your house?

–Let's see, let's plan something; tell me the things he likes to do besides drinking beer.

–He likes going to rock concerts and playing tennis.

–Excellent, we'll take him to play tennis every day until he's completely worn out and has no more strength left to try something with you.

–But, what am I going to do with him all day in my house!

–You're going to have to take him out; didn't you invite him to see the flowery desert?

Among all her friends they planned a very busy schedule of activities; the idea was to keep him busy outside the house so that when he arrived at night, he would be too tired, only wanting to go to sleep. That's how they organized barbecues, walks on the beach, excursions to the desert and walks in vineyards, however, the celebrations of September 18th were only lasting a week and then her friends would have to return to work, ending the help and valuable company that they were going to give her. One of her most daring and jealous friend said:

–I'm going to bring you a gun so you can keep it under your pillow and, if he tries anything, you just shoot him; it'll be in self-defence. And you can lock yourself in your room and even sleep with your clothes on if it makes you feel safer.

The unexpected date arrived, at least for Esmeralda, because Terry instead, only desired to see her and, was taking a risk by trying to win her love. What better proof of love than travelling from London to Copiapó, at the end of the world, in a distant place, just to see his beloved princess. Around noon, he called to tell her that he had arrived safely in Santiago, Chile, and was waiting for the flight to Copiapó and, she replied in a concise and cold way:

–Hello, I'll see you at the Atacama Desert airport.

She hung up the phone without even saying goodbye or asking how he had arrived.

By not having any interest in seeing him or receiving his visit, she didn't try to arrive early at the airport, she only organized her work schedule in the city of Copiapó to be able to dress casual and not with work clothes. It got late and she arrived thirty minutes after the plane had landed and, since the airport was so small it couldn't have taken him more than ten minutes to get off and retrieve his luggage. It was noticeable that he was very eager to see her, he saw her arrive and rushed to hug her, Esmeralda however tried to get away as soon as possible, saying:

–I'm sorry, I was working.

–Don't worry about it.

–What would you like to do?

–Anything, whatever you decide, I'm a very easy-going person.

– Hearing him say "I'm a very easy-going person who can accommodate to anything," made her want to laugh ironically, taking into account how stressed she had been with his unexpected visit, at least for her; however, she had to bite her tongue and behave like a young lady, responding:

–Would you like to go to the beach to see Bahía Inglesa and have lunch?

–Oh, yes! That's a perfect idea.

On the way to Bahía Inglesa, little by little they let loose and Esmeralda began to behave relatively more friendly, he spoke more, telling her how the trip had been and how surprised he was to see the desert from the plane, absolutely dry, arid, empty, without any greenery and, suddenly when the plane approached Caldera the appearance of the landscape completely changed; he was enthralled with the colourful majesty of the flowers covering much of the desert.

They walked along the beach; it was more beautiful than ever. Esmeralda with pride in her Atacameña land and its wonderful beaches said smiling and in a boastful tone:

–These are real beaches, with crystal clear waters and sand, not like yours that look like chocolate because of how dirty they are –she said exaggerating and laughing like a witty little girl.

–Bahía Inglesa is very beautiful, ah, but the water is so cold, not like the Mediterranean.

–As far as I know, the water in England isn't from the Mediterranean, it's like if I compared the temperature of Chilean beaches to the ones in Mexico or San Andres, Colombia, they're absolutely different; don't you think? Anyway, it's time for lunch.

Before embarking on the trip to *Copiapó,* they took a last walk along the beach, the water looked exquisite, ideal for taking a dip, but even if it hadn't been so hot, she wasn't going to get in the water because she didn't want to be seen in a bathing suit. It was a spring day, without tourists, he was fascinated, although his tiredness was noticeable. When they arrived home, Esmeralda showed him to his room, telling him to leave his luggage and to get ready to go out, adding:

–We're invited to dinner at one of my friend's house; it's Alejandrina's birthday and she speaks English, so it'll be ideal for you to integrate and chat.

–Thanks, I was thinking of going to sleep.

–I'm sorry; you'll be able to rest and sleep when we get back.

She was cold and very serious; you could say almost rude. On the contrary, despite being tired, he complied with humility and infinite sweetness, completely unaware of what awaited him and the sinister plan that the mischievous Esmeralda had prepared for him, who scared as she was, would do everything in her power in order to defend her honour.

It was the week of national holiday celebrations in Chile, everyone was celebrating and, it was very easy to share at friends' houses around a delicious barbecue or empanadas, in addition to official government holidays such as parades, military parade and Ramadas (establishments for Chilean national holidays), where you could enjoy and dance to the beat of folk music, taste the typical Chilean cuisine and, visit the artisanal fairs and popular games, Native sports, which are indigenous sports of Chile such as taming animals and the traditional September 18th mining rodeo. When they arrived home, effectively exhausted from so much walking, sharing, eating and drinking, they were ready to fall asleep, although he managed to try and say good night with a kiss on the cheek, while Esmeralda locked herself under seven keys in her bedroom and dragged one of the nightstands by the door, to be able to wake up by the sound of it dragging across the floor in case he dared to open it. When the festivities were over and, having visited all the possible tourist places there were and, even repeating the visits to the flowery desert and to the beach, Esmeralda began to worry as she saw him more relaxed, smiling and gaining confidence and, she was without knowing where else to take him and what else to do. To all this, her friends, those who didn't know the behind the scenes of the UK man's visit, as they called him with affection, asked if they were a couple and, when answering no, they would make jokes saying that they looked good together, that they could form a beautiful couple even offering to be godparents at their wedding, to which Esmeralda would respond by frowning and showing annoyance. There were other friends who went further with their comments and insinuations, like her friend Priscila, who came up with a brilliant idea, although absolutely inappropriate in the circumstances in which Esmeralda found herself:

–Esmeralda, why don't you take him on holidays to the south, like to La Serena? You can't keep him trapped here in Copiapó, ugly as it is.

–No, how dare you, Prici! It's not necessary, we have beautiful beaches here.

–But you already took him to the beach, didn't you?

–Yes, but we can keep walking around; we still have to visit Chañaral.

–Chañaral? Why are you taking him to Chañaral? That beach is contaminated with tailings. Stop all your foolishness and take him to visit Viña del Mar.

Terry seemed enthusiastic about the idea and, asked Priscila and Marcelo where these places were, how to get there and what they could visit. And they hallucinated telling him the tourist wonders, exaggerating the descriptions of each place. Poor Esmeralda, the next day when she got up, he was sitting down serving himself a cup of coffee and some toasts, he was used to getting up early because of the five-hour difference between Chile and the United Kingdom and, due to the high summer temperatures, to which he wasn't used to. He looked at her with great joy and enthusiasm and told her his plan:

–Esmi, I would love to go and visit the places your friend Priscila and Marcelo suggested…

She was in shock and before he could continue, she abruptly interrupted him by replying:

–No, we can't go, I'm sorry.

–Why not?

–Because I don't have a job, I have classes at the university and have no money. If you want to go, then go by yourself.

–How, if I don't know Chile? I wouldn't be able to travel alone, apart from the fact that I don't know how to speak Spanish, I also want to spend time with you; I came to Chile to see and be with you.

She left him speaking alone as she turned around and went to the bathroom to shower. When she came out, he kept insisting and she responded?

–Ok, fine, if you want me to join you, let's go, but I only dispose of my time and car; if you want to go you're going to have to pay for everything, from the fuel to the accommodations.

–That's fine, tell me how much is the cost of fuel, the hotel room and how much we'd spend approximately on food.

–Mmm, the gasoline isn't expensive, don't worry about that, but the toll charges are, although that isn't either, it's not a lot, what is expensive though is the hotel room.

–How much is a hotel room?

–Mmm, around $100.000 a night and we'll need two rooms, one for each of us and, food isn't too expensive, let's say another $100.000 per day, aside from drinks –she said, bulging the figures and in a triumphant tone, she was sure that he was going to find it very expensive and would give up the idea.

As she came out of her bedroom, Terry was waiting for her with pencil and paper on hand and, he said in a winning tone:

–Yes, I have drawn up the numbers of how much money we'll need for the trip down south and, I can afford it, don't worry about the money, what do you think about leaving tomorrow?

–Tomorrow???????

Things were becoming difficult and, her friends would mock her by saying:

–You can't save yourself from this one, my friend, mmm, holidays in *La Serena* and in Viña del Mar, pouring yourself an exquisite pisco sour –a typical cocktail of Chilean gastronomy made with pisco and lemon – on the edge of the ocean while watching a sunset or enjoying a warm summer night... impossible, nothing can stop this.

That was the kind of joke they made, making fun of poor Esmeralda for being so naive, while she, at this point in Terry's visit, had to go with the punches. Indeed, as it had been announced, the prophecy was beginning to come true and she was resisting with all her might. On their first stop in the beautiful city of La Serena, bursting with colour and packed with tourists, with infinite bars and restaurants on Avenida del Mar and the Peñuelas casino, an environment ideal for enjoying a wonderful holiday as a couple, he had been managing without any luck up to that point. Esmeralda, on her behalf, had managed to avoid him. After three days in La Serena, they continued their trip to *Santiago;* Esmeralda with a winning smile stretched her neck and, opening the car door, asked:

–Are you driving, or am I?

He responded serene:

–Whatever you want.

–In that case then you're driving, I want to rest and read my emails.

Happy with the first stage over, she submerged herself in her phone telling her friends how the trip was going, they laughed responding: don't claim victory ahead of time. When they arrived in *Santiago,* they had a problem with the reservations, something had happened with the credit card, the transaction had been rejected and the hotel had no available rooms. They began the task of looking for a new hotel, finding one that had only one room; he, smiling and taking advantage of the situation told the person who attended them:

–Perfect, I'll take the room.

To which Esmeralda furiously replied:

–No, we're not going to stay in one room, we need two.

–But how, aren't you a couple? You look so good together.

Fuming and tired of looking for hotels, she took her bag and stormed out of the reception. Luckily, the adjoining hotel had available rooms, although much more expensive, $150,000 each, –yes, give us two, please–, and looked at Terry gesturing to pay.

That night was exhausting, she locked herself in her room crying with rage, she was tired, she couldn't take it anymore and, she didn't even join him for dinner. After two days of visiting the most tourist places in *Santiago*, they headed to the countryside, to her parents' house in Pichidegua, where he was received like a king, everyone was fascinated with him. Esmeralda's parents went out of their way to attend him, he spent hours with her father playing dominoes and drinking red wine and beer, time that she took advantage of to rest and visit her aunts, cousins and friends from the countryside. She didn't always invite him to accompany her, he was happy being with her parents, becoming even jealous of how well they were treating him and the time they were spending with him talking, because in the countryside no one could speak English, least of all her parents and siblings.

From there they went to Viña del Mar, once again she felt like she was drowning and no longer wanted to be in his presence. She called her friend Irina and they met up at a bar located in front of the hotel, with whom she unburdened herself by telling her how terrible of a time she was having. She felt sorry for her and listened carefully, trying to help, in that Irina looked up staring at the man who was approaching her table, it was Terry, who greeted her and asked Esmeralda why she had left him alone without letting him know, to which she responded:

–I didn't want to bother you; the important thing is that you're here; what do you want to drink?

–A beer, please, *Crystal* –he loved *Crystal* beer.

As soon as he got up to go to the bathroom, Irina approached her friend asking with great curiosity:

–But, what don't you like about him? He's great, he seems super nice, respectful and you can tell he's hopelessly in love with you, don't be so mean, give him a chance.

–No, I don't want anything with any man, not with him nor anyone else.

–Ay, and what about Todd?

–Well, that's something else.

–But, my friend, look at him, he's so sweet, don't let the opportunity pass by, you'll regret it later.

–Keep him; you can have him if you find him so interesting.

–No, it's not like that, I'm single and I'd love to be in a relationship again, but I've had really bad luck. But that's how life is; you have men chasing you and I'm here searching for scraps.

–Shut up and stop talking nonsense, he's coming over.

Her friend Irina was of great help, company and salvation; they walked around together, she took them to the Prat Pier, the Paseo 21 de Mayo, to Olmué, they visited an infinity of tourist places. They were wonderful days spent with her friend Irina, not with Terry, as she said in a triumphant and witty tone.

Back in Copiapó, Terry had the opportunity to meet Apollo and Renata, not Victoria, who flatly refused to share with him, telling her mother that she didn't want to meet her lovers and, that if she wanted to visit Viccencito she had to go alone, because she wasn't going to let him into her home. And so it was, every time Esmeralda went to visit her grandson, Terry had to wait for her in the car two blocks away. During Terry's last days in Copiapó, Esmeralda had resumed her work and studies; he went with her to several of her educational seminars and was of great help and companionship, as well as getting to know the work she did. Another important event that occurred in Chile in those days was the whole movement related to the accident at the San José mine, a fact that she had explained in great detail when she got to know the inside of the mine and the vast majority of the workers trapped at 700 meters deep. Everyone commented on the news with great sorrow, praying and pleading that they could be rescued safe and sound as soon as possible, and so it was, the 33 miners came to the surface of the mine reuniting with their families.

His visit generated some very peculiar and anecdotal events, such as, for example, his name: Terry, in Chile, is a very common name for dogs, making Esmeralda uncomfortable and, even worse was when they went to a friend's house whose pet's name coincidently was Terry. She remembers that they were happily sharing at a barbecue, every day they were invited to share, one after another, celebrations of the 18th with empanadas and abundant and exquisite barbecues, that is how while they were in the backyard getting ready to sit at the table, Dany yelled in discomfort:

–Terry, leave, get out of here, you're not invited to the barbecue.

Terry looked at Esmeralda very scared and with his face disfigured asked:

–What happened? What did I do wrong, why is your friend so furious with me?

–Sorry, sorry, sorry, Terry! –Dany exclaimed embarrassed addressing Terry and then Esmeralda, adding:

–Esmi, Esmi, I'm sorry, can you explain to Terry that I wasn't yelling at him? Tell him, please, that my dog's name is also Terry.

They couldn't stop laughing after explaining to Terry what had happened and, every time the puppy showed up, they would quietly call him: buddy, buddy...

Regarding dogs, Terry was extremely struck by the number of dogs and even more so, by the fact that they were on the streets without their owners; he managed to count up to ten dogs in one block, something that was unusual for her, unfortunately when trying to prove otherwise, she counted an average of eight stray dogs and on a couple of occasions even more than twelve and, it wasn't because they were chasing a dog in heat.

Celebratory barbecues for September 18th

Terry made a very important change in his diet before travelling to Chile, when he was warned that in Chile, they ate a lot of meat and, for the celebration of national holidays, all the families would make barbecues, *anticuchos* (meat brochette) and empanadas. It would be important to prepare for that situation, because he was a vegetarian: before travelling he began to eat meat and thus in Chile he joined in on the celebrations without major difficulties.

In relation to leaving him tired by playing tennis, he only played twice, it was impossible to schedule more tennis matches, everyone was partying, nobody wanted anything to do with sports or exercise until after September 18th, yes, because that's when everyone wanted to lose weight and get in shape to prepare for a summer without a shirt, however, Terry had gone on holiday to the south and on his return, he accompanied Esmeralda to her field trips, the days flying by and not having time to play tennis.

Another tragicomic situation that happened with Terry was that the day before his return to England, he needed to buy a razor and other things at the supermarket. That night Esmeralda had classes at the university and was late, so she left him at the supermarket previously explaining to him how to get home. Classes were from seven to eleven at night and, that day as soon as the class ended, she quickly went home without sharing with her classmates, as they would usually do and even go out to a bar for a couple of drinks. When she arrived home, she was surprised to find Terry outside, cold, wearing a shirt and shorts, and asked him with great concern:

–What happened, why are you outside? Why didn't you go inside the house?

–Because you forgot to leave me the keys.

Her guy friends continued to complain when they saw her and when they learned that she was walking around with her UK friend everywhere and, that she had even taken him to Viña del Mar, they called reproaching her:

–How is it possible, I'm your friend and you haven't even extended me an invitation to have tea at your house, and you have that stranger sleeping in your home?

–He's leaving soon, don't worry.

Indeed, Esmeralda was very reserved about the people she invited into her home, a couple of friends and eventually larger groups when celebrating special occasions, but the only men who entered her home were the delivery guys of liquefied gas, water and the ones who measured the consumption of water and electricity.

Esmeralda behaved very cold towards him practically during the three weeks that he visited and shared with her, even his farewell was very sad. That morning, he got surprised to the point that tears rolled down his cheeks when he saw Esmeralda coming out of the bedroom still in her pyjamas, as it was time to go to the airport, and he heard her say:

–Terry, your taxi has just arrived; it's outside waiting for you.

–You're not coming with me to the airport?

–Sorry, I have a meeting and if I go with you, I won't make it back on time.

They shared a big hug and, without saying a single word, said goodbye. Terry left and she returned to bed, giving a sigh of great relief, but at the same time she was invaded by great sadness, it had affected her seeing him leave so sad and crying.

CHAPTER V

A trip to London in search of... a second chance

The years 2011 and 2012 flew by for Esmeralda, the hours of the day weren't enough for her to deal with and respond to her master's studies and work responsibilities; each day demanded more time and travel, not only on the mining sites in Atacama, but also to the regions of Coquimbo and La Serena, which implied travelling and staying up to three days away from home, doing field work and in the city promoting the company's pharmaceutical chemical line. What was entertaining about her job, was the dynamism and the different scenarios, work and professional areas in which she worked, enjoying the landscape, travelling, and as always, combining work with pleasure, a very typical phrase of Esmeralda referring to enjoying her work and taking advantage of the opportunity that travelling offered her, such as getting a snack on the road at a typical Chilean restaurant that serves food with large portions at affordable prices, tasting a delicious *Locos con salsa verde*

(Chilean abalone with green sauce) in La Ovallina, serving herself an exquisite entrecote in Bavaria or a common sole with capers and white sauce in one of the most famous restaurants on Avenida del Mar in La Serena, or taking a stroll around the Peñuelas casino to serve herself a delicious whisky while trying her luck at the slot machines. Ah! But the most extraordinary thing was to change her security clothing for her bathing suit and go diving in Villa Alegre and Bahía Inglesa. Visiting her daughter and spoiling her grandson was what filled her heart and soul with love.

Due to her great social sensitivity and love for others, she was very active in her volunteer service at the Copiapó Lions Club, and as a firefighter in the Copiapó Fire Department she was part of La Pompa Italia, an association of volunteer firefighters founded by the Italian community. Regarding the role of firefighter and, since not everything is easy in life, she had to face a serious health diagnosis: she was doing honour guard next to a fellow firefighter's coffin, who had died as a result of uterine cancer that had been detected late, when it was already in a metastatic state. During those four hours on duty, she prayed a lot and also made a promise to the deceased young woman, that she would sensitize her friends into getting a Pap test in order to be treated ahead of time if they were to be positive, starting with herself. She had the test done and after a couple of weeks, she remembered that she hadn't gone to retrieve the results. She was alone, wearing her mining outfit; that day she had gone down early and, very naturally she opened the envelope as if it were any ordinary letter. It was a great shock when she found a positive diagnosis, news that unsettled her and, the image of her co-worker inside the coffin stuck in her mind without being able to shake it off. She crossed the street and sat on a bench in Copiapó's Plaza de Armas, and read and re-read the certificate with the test results: it was a grade two cancer, treatable. However, the word cancer is automatically and mistakenly associated with death; she took a deep breath and called her midwife friend Jessica, who gave her emotional support and reassured her that it was absolutely treatable and that there was nothing to worry about. She suggested visiting a trusted and prestigious gynecologist in Copiapó, to verify the veracity of the test and start medical treatment immediately.

After visiting the doctor, who offered to do the surgery and treatment, she thought about it and made the decision to travel to Santiago and be treated at an oncology centre. Despite her strength and ability to face situations of great difficulty and pain, she had to face cancer all alone; Victoria was worried about finishing her university studies and raising her son, while Apollo and Renata were submerged in their own affairs. She was staying at her beloved aunt Carmencita's house. She received all the love and support from her aunt and cousins and, the day she had to go in for surgery was emotionally very painful: she had to arrive at seven in the morning, she went alone and, when checking in, they asked her for her companions signature, a person who they would turn to in case of, she responded in a guttural voice:

–It's just me –without being able to avoid it, the tears started flowing and, she began to feel faint; the professional who was attending her, took her hand and handed her a box of tissues, kindly saying:

–Calm down, don't worry, everything will be fine, the doctors here are excellent and you will recover in no time.

What really broke her heart was the lack of support from her loved ones; having cancer was a secondary issue.

–Tell me, is there anyone you would like us to call? You can give us any number, it's only in case of; it's necessary, it's the clinic's policies.

–No, I don't have anyone, it's just me and, my mother who I could turn to, but she's old and I don't want to cause any problems, she already has enough of her own.

–Think of a friend perhaps.

She thought about her midwife friends, Jessica and Cecilia, she finally gave him the name and number of a priest, her spiritual guide.

When she woke up from surgery and found herself alone on a gurney surrounded by blue folding screens that looked like paper, still somnolent from the effects of the anesthetic, she burst into tears wondering why, why was she alone, why weren't her children with her, why had they abandoned her in her worst moments. It was a cluster of mixed feelings, because on the other hand, she felt that she deserved such cruel and insensitive treatment from her children for not having been able to keep the family together, feeling tremendously guilty thinking that she had nothing to ask of them and even more so keeping in mind that according to them, she had abandoned them, however it had been her ex-husband who had manipulated the facts in his favour, denying her the house that she had requested to take her three children to live with her, he instead had preferred to rent it and thus avoid Esmeralda from claiming it, knowing that the children wouldn't go and live in her recently purchased house because it was very small, with only two bedrooms. Basically, the rejection was based on her location, in a neighbourhood that was not up to par and the level that they were accustomed to, being the children of a general manager of a large mining company. All those thoughts ran in circles and rumbled in her head, it was so much pain, bitterness and suffering that she only wanted to die. At that moment, she felt a tender hand wiping her tears and heard a soft voice:

–Esmeraldita, Esmeraldita, don't cry, everything went great, I've already spoken to the doctors, everything is OK, there's nothing to worry about.

Her cousin Isabel was the angel that had arrived to save her and make her react. The next day, she felt more composed, rejoicing with the visit of her mother and older sister, as well as three of her dear friends, including her colleagues and friends from university Lissette and *Anita la guerrillera* (the warrior) –with much affection, respect and admiration she called her la *guerrillera* because of her passion and dedication in fighting in favour of social causes, being common to see her leading social mobilizations and strikes on behalf of health professionals, since she worked in that area of expertise–.

Upon her return to *Copiapó*, she continued to feel emotionally fragile, lacking in affection, love and protection. Who would have guessed, being so strong, bold and independent! But every person has their weak side, their weak point. Her little grandson Viccencito and the soon arrival of her second grandson, fed her with love and joy, while she and her neighbour and friend Lina supported each other; every night they got together to talk, play cards and drink. There were months when they drank a lot and also smoked, while her other neighbour Elsita took care of her and spoiled her. God blessed and protected her by putting guardian angels in her life, in her case, he sent her an army of his angels and spread them everywhere, wherever he wanted them to go. One of them was her neighbour Elsita, always concerned about her health and well-being, taking care of her as if she were her daughter, she even watered her front lawn; she treated her with exquisite dishes of homemade food, such as a good plate of ossobuco casserole, *porotos granados (*Chilean stew with beans, corn and pumpkin) and, chicken with peas and mashed potatoes. How would she not remember when she asked for their help in those days and nights of panic and anxiety attacks, in which she felt crazy from the sensation of lacking air, suffocated and sweaty; Elsita would sit next to her bed and calm her with her sweetness, prayers and words of encouragement, and wouldn't leave until she saw her asleep.

One Sunday morning, she was kneeling down, praying and imploring God for the closeness and love of her children. She was suffering a lot because the relationships with her daughter Victoria had become very tense, she wasn't allowing her to see her little grandson, causing her a heart breaking pain; in those moments the sweet, tender and loving image of Terry appeared in her thoughts. That image invaded her thoughts day and night, his presence was becoming stronger and she couldn't decipher what it was. They had stopped communicating; they had known nothing about each other for practically two years. In the middle of her prayers, Terry's face appeared once again, each time more tangible; she reacted by asking God:

–My God, I've always asked you to give me back the love of my children and the company of your angels, however, today I see that you have sent me one of your angels that wasn't in my plans, I even rejected him and was cruel to him.

Smiling, she did the sign of the cross and began to breathe with new vigour and experience feelings of love and happiness. Every time she remembered Terry, she wondered and answered herself, as if she were conversing with God:

–You sent him to me, I appreciate it and the idea is beginning to excite me.

Her days began to flourish and she began to remember every situation she had experienced during his visit to Chile, how much her friends had told her that they made a beautiful couple, she thought about why she hadn't tried and what hadn't she liked about him. She realized, that she had never allowed herself a second to look at him as a man, as a potential partner, as her life partner, she only protected herself by creating a great inescapable barrier between the two, an invincible wall without even giving him a smile. Recapitulating, she smiled mischievously and flirtatiously, saying to herself:

–Mmm, to be honest the UK man is pretty good looking.

And she took the liberty of writing him an email, but reacted thinking that more than two years had passed and, what could have happened to his life, perhaps he had even gotten married. She decided to write to him anyway, briefly and very directly:

... "Dear Terry, I hope you're doing well, I know it's been a while since the last time we wrote to each other. I'm sorry for not being kinder to you when you came to visit me, I'm really sorry, but I wasn't ready to start a new love relationship, but I am now. So, if you want and are single, we could try" ...

In response, she received a very affectionate email and better than she had expected, he was still single, working, enjoying rock music and playing tennis, his two children were fine and, most importantly, he was single.

From that day on, the emails were daily and each time they became more affectionate and thus, a genuine love relationship was born, well, he was in love with Esmeralda and, she was finally giving herself the opportunity to live love for the second time. They treated each other as a couple, they began to miss each other and planned a second visit, which this time would be Esmeralda's turn to travel to his home in London.

They were adults and independent, they organized the trip and Esmeralda flew to London for three weeks. During that time, they shared and lived to the fullest, both absolutely attuned, happy, enjoying each other's company, united by love. He made use of his two weeks holiday to share with Esmeralda, dedicating himself entirely to spoiling her and going out, as he knew of her taste in whisky and Scottish music, surprising her with a trip to Edinburgh. She projected great happiness and radiant energy, enjoyed everything and in particular the love and passion for Scottish music and folklore; she was irresistibly attracted to the music of a bagpipe, every time she heard one, no matter how far it was, she would run to watch and enjoy the show. Touring Edinburgh, she heard a piper, took Terry's hand and hurried to where the artist was playing; enthralled she stopped in front of him, delighting in the magical melody of the bagpipes. She remembered a tradition that she had read and heard about the Scots and, in particular, what the pipers did; so doing one of her antics and wanting to find out, she asked Terry:

–Is it true that pipers don't wear underpants? –making a bad girls face and smiling in a mischievous way.

–I don't know, why are you asking that? –he responded with a strange face.

–Because I've read that they don't usually wear underpants under those Scottish skirts, kilts –with a pleading face she asked–: Please! Can you ask him if he's wearing underpants or not?

Terry blushed even more and said categorically:

–No! How dare you, I can't ask that!

–Ok, in that case I'll ask him myself.

She approached the piper, who had stopped playing to take a break, she asked him balancing her body like a little girl from side to side and her hands together:

–Excuse me, can I ask you a question?

–Yes, of course, what is it?

The piper answered with absolute naturalness and kindly; absolute innocence from what Esmeralda was about to ask. She got closer to him, put her hands around his ear and stepping on her tip toes to reach his height, asked:

–Are you wearing underpants?

The man backed away extremely shocked and red as a tomato and, stuttering replied:

–Excuse me, what are you asking me?

–I want to know if it's true that pipers don't wear underpants.

–Yes, the tradition is to not wear underpants when we dress with our Scottish skirt called kilt.

He lowered his voice and ducked down to be at Esmeralda's height adding:

–But to be honest, today I wore underpants because it's really cold outside.

She responded in a low voice as well as him:

–Ok, thank you very much. It'll be our little secret –placing her right index finger on her lips gesturing silence.

–Yes, our little secret –making the same gesture and grabbing the bagpipe to continue playing, while Esmeralda moved away almost dragged by Terry, who was dying of more embarrassment than the piper.

One of her antics, putting Terry in a tight spot

That was how spontaneous and mischievous Esmeralda was, the most unlikely things occurred to her, such as approaching the guards at Buckingham Palace asking to be escorted to Queen Elizabeth II's quarters because she was invited to have tea with her.

Terry's children, two young adults of twenty-one and twenty-three years old, received her well, although they didn't share much, because they were used to coming from their jobs and locking themselves in their rooms to play video games; it was their way of being, super independent, each one prepared their own meal and went up with their trays to their rooms, only a couple of times they agreed to join their father and Esmeralda for dinner. While all of Terry's friends wanted to meet her, they invited them to bars to enjoy rock bands and gigs. It was said that Latin women were well received and loved by the English for their beauty, happiness, sympathy, long black hair and for their way of being, which Esmeralda could affirm was indeed true. On the other hand, both Terry's father and brother also welcomed her very well, with them they shared a Sunday roast dinner, a typical Sunday English lunch. A very special event was Esmeralda's fiftieth birthday celebration in the events room of the Elm Park tennis club of which Terry was a member; he had organized a wonderful party, even with a DJ and an open bar, there were many of Terry's friends, about a hundred people, friends from work, rock, and obviously his family and friends with whom he played tennis, as well as a couple of Esmeralda's friends from her time as an English student.

During the stay at Terry's house, Esmeralda presented two asthma attacks, having to resort to the indiscriminate use of inhalers and even take antibiotics, thinking that it could have been a product of the winter cold in England and the trip to Scotland. No, the crises had been due to Terry's pet, a beautiful cat who slept on his bed, obviously during the days of her visit the cat was put in another room, away from her, to avoid the asthmatic reaction, but the hairs and mites were all over the place and especially on the bed. That was a complex subject to discuss.

After the two weeks of holidays, he returned to work, and Esmeralda was home alone, but took the time to visit some of her friends, her Lions friends, Hepzibah, and one of her favourite teachers, Miss Pamela, from her English school, which she had visited to greet her other teachers and administrative staff. She met Terry in downtown London and they enjoyed a couple of Scottish whiskies at a bar, which had to be different from the last time; she had asked him to go to a different bar every time they went out, which was very easy to do, because in England there are countless bars, taverns and pubs, one on each corner, and in London there are hundreds, one next to the other.

When Terry went to work and she was left alone, she imagined what her life would be like living with him, at home, and she began to play the role of house owner without saying anything to him. She would get up, clean, tidy up, change the position of the furniture and place fresh flowers on the dining room table and air freshener, leaving everything spotless and then going out for a stroll; and when she'd stay home, she'd cook and wait for him with an exquisite dinner. He looked very happy with Esmeralda's presence in his house.

With two days left before returning to Chile, she felt that she was going to miss him very much; she had had such a great time with him, that she didn't want to leave and have everything ended or have their relationship turned into a long distance one, supported by emails and video calls. On the other hand, she felt a sinner, she felt that it wasn't correct to have shared three weeks with him as a couple and then leave as if nothing had happened, no, that couldn't be, that didn't sit well with her, she would never do that, she wasn't a "touch and go" kind of person, she didn't want a temporary relationship, besides, it had cost her so much to accept it. The day before her trip; she asked him to take her to Kensington Palace, although she had visited it on countless occasions, she wanted to go again, she felt it was a very special place because Lady Diana had lived in that palace, her presence and energy was still felt in furniture, walls, curtains and, particularly in the exhibitions of her dresses and in the palace gardens, which were wonderful. Upon reaching the park and before entering the palace, Esmeralda playing around said to Terry:

–Whoever sees the first squirrel gets to make a wish and, whoever loses, has to grant it.

Accepting the challenge, both began a frantic search to see the first squirrel; it was very difficult to see one, probably because it was a place frequented by hundreds of tourists and because of the time of year, the middle of English winter. Terry was lucky enough to see a squirrel first, but said that he would make his wish known later. After visiting the palace and touring the park, they went to have lunch at an English pub located in front of one of the main entrances of the park, called Pub Goat Tavern. When they finished lunch, they saw the coins in the change and, they commented on the different types of coins, making the comparison between the value of pounds in Chile and pesos in England; she got up from the table excusing herself to go to the bathroom, and on returning, Terry, very smiling and nervous, took her by the hands and looking into her eyes asked her:

–Do you want to marry me?

–Yes!!! –She instantly responded, with great joy and almost screaming with emotion, it was exactly what she had wanted to hear and even if he hadn't asked, she would have been willing to ask him to marry her. That had been her goal with the bet on who saw the first squirrel.

They kissed and hugged with much passion, joy and euphoria; they both wanted it and were ready to get married. He confessed that in the week he had been working, he had imagined every day how life would be like with her if they were married, he loved that she would receive him so happy when he returned from work, with a big smile, a kiss and a hug, saying:

–I'm so glad you're home, I missed you so much.

He loved that the house smelled like home, with her presence it was different, everything shined and it was joy. She told him that she had done the same exercise of imagining living together and that she had loved the experience, although she would only have added to it having a good job, because she didn't like to be at home all day.

Before leaving the bar, they had already planned to get married as soon as possible, in three months, first in Chile and then in England, and they had agreed that she would prepare and organize the wedding in Chile and he in England.

The 21st century prince

CHAPTER VI

Preparations for the wedding ceremony and wedding night and the outrageous deportation from Heathrow airport

Upon her return to Santiago, Chile, as soon as she arrived at the Arturo Merino Benítez airport, she got access to the internet and immediately called her friend Verónica; after greeting her, she asked her to reserve her company's event room for her marriage celebration, who incredulously and in shock responded:

–You're kidding me?

–No, no, not at all, you know I went to London to meet Terry's family, the English man that came to visit me for September 18th, do you remember I invited him to see the flowery desert?

–Yes, I remember you wanted nothing to do with him, or did you change your mind?

–Not exactly, it's not that I changed my mind, it's just that I was defensive and didn't want anything to do with any man, well, finally I realized that it could happen and I love it, I love him and we're going to get married.

–Are you crazy? How can you think that an English man is going to travel from England to Chile just to marry you? No, my friend, please, react, open your eyes, you're no longer a little girl that believes everything she is told.

–Verito, I'm going to get married, whether you believe it or not.

–My friend, I'm just advising you, I don't want to see you cry and even less suffer.

–Thanks, my friend, I know you love me and want the best for me and, I thank you from the bottom of my heart, that's why I want you to help me organize my wedding.

–My friend, when you arrive to Copiapó, come to my house so we can chat.

–Please Verito, if you don't believe me and don't want to make the reservation at your company, I'll have to choose another location for my wedding.

–It's not about that, Esmeralda, I can make the reservation, but I insist that we need to talk first.

–Talk about what? There's nothing to talk about, just tell me what dates you have available in May.

–Mmm, let me check my calendar…what about the first week of May?

–No, that's too early, what about the last Saturday of May?

–In that case, it should be the first week of June.

–Ok, perfect, thanks, my friend, as soon as I arrive to Copiapó, after visiting my daughter Victoria and giving my little grandson Vinccencito his gifts, I'll come to your house. Alright, bye, bye! I have to get off the plane.

Esmeralda laughed alone, she felt so happy that she wanted to share this with everyone, tell her friends, co-workers, her neighbour Elsita and her friend Lina, because she knew they would be very happy with her news. She was worried about the reaction of her children, she wondered how they would take the news of her marriage and the fact that she would be moving to London. It was such a complex issue that she had to look for the right moment, but by taking her time she also ran the risk of them finding out through someone else, although she saw this as very difficult and almost impossible since they moved in different circles.

That weekend, she went to the beach for a walk with a couple of friends, taking the opportunity to book the wedding night at the Hotel Rocas de Bahía, being the perfect place to spend the wedding night and enjoy her last weekend by the ocean, before setting out on a trip to England to start her new life as a remarried woman, with the certainty that a second marriage would be better than the first. The hotel receptionist took her to see the Premier Suite and; she was amazed at the spectacular beach view that it had, she could even see it lying in bed, the view from the terrace was dreamy, allowing her to see and enjoy both the sunset and the sunrise The room was spacious, very comfortable, decorated with exquisite finesse and delicacy, ideal for a wedding night, it even had a jacuzzi, showing a small flaw that would be repaired.

Esmeralda was very detailed and had exquisite tastes, she took care of including in the room reservation everything necessary in order to ensure a dream wedding night; she asked for it to be decorated with white and red roses, have chocolates, champagne and grapes, in addition to having the room tempered at the time of their arrival – which, she calculated, would be between three and four in the morning–. She ended the visit at the hotel, paying in advance the reservation, even though it wasn't necessary, but she wanted to leave everything paid for to feel free, without any worries so she could dedicate herself fully and exclusively to enjoying the love of her husband. That afternoon, as she walked along the shoreline, barefoot, enjoying the gentle lapping of the waves on her tiny feet, she laughed and hallucinated telling her friends how wonderful her trip to London had been and how much fun she had had. They laughed a lot and made fun of how stupid she had been to reject Terry when he had visited her, feeling sorry for him.

Her friends from a TV channel also greeted her very happily, Benjamin stood out for the high quality of his photographic work and Francisco Droguet was a brilliant cameraman, he worked for the local government, in addition to providing professional services to TVN and to his own channel. When she saw them, she was happy to say hello and tell them that she was going to get married and that she would love to hire their services to cover her wedding. They congratulated her and gladly accepted the challenge.

Due to work, she travelled to Santiago and, that was the perfect occasion and opportunity to break the news of her marriage to her son Apollo and Renata. She invited them to dinner and, being now in a more trusting and relaxed atmosphere, she commented with great joy that she had great news to tell them. Without preamble, she gave them the news in one big breath:

–I'm getting married and moving to England.

Faced with the news, Renata reacted super well and was very happy:

–Really, mum? You're going to marry the English man that came to visit you for the 18th?

–Yes, I'm going to marry Terry –Esmeralda responded euphoric.

–Ah! That's great! I liked him a lot, he seems really nice and outgoing –she added while laughing–, and he likes rock music just like me.

On the contrary, Apollo reacted really upset:

–No, mum, you can't get married, mum, you can't get married again...! –Renata and her mother interrupted him with questioning curiosity, speaking at the same time and raising their voice:

–And why not?

–No, you can't get married, you're already married, you already married dad once.

–But, son, your father and I have been separated for four years and, we even got divorced.

–Ah, I don't know, but you can't get married, that's all I'm saying.

With Apollo opposed to his mother's marriage, the conversation turned more tense, despite that she and Renata were trying to clear the air, without being able to achieve it.

With respect to Victoria, she took the news with absolute indifference, as if it were none of her business. At first, she refused to attend the wedding, worried about her father's reaction, who would surely be angry with her if she participated in her mother's event. Near the wedding date, she agreed on going with the condition that Esmeralda would have to pay for her dress and the children's outfits as a flower girl and ring bearer, to which Esmeralda agreed. On the other hand, Esmeralda's friends were extremely happy, they dreamed of their friend's happiness, aware of her past and unfortunate marriage; she deserved to be happy and what better than with Terry, also they had all tried to unite them as a couple without succeeding, until she decided to give herself a second chance in search of happiness.

They were three very intense months for Esmeralda, there were many things to prepare and do and make big decisions, not only regarding the wedding organization, which was already a lot, but also everything related to moving abroad, thinking about what she would do with her home, with her furniture, her car, quitting her job, although she had already experienced that with her first study trip to London; but now it was totally different. She was moving to another country, to another continent, with an absolutely different culture and very far from all her loved ones. Her greatest pain was knowing she wouldn't be able to see her grandchildren, it was no longer just her adorable Viccencito, the family had grown, her grandson had a little sister, the sweet and beautiful little princess Doménica; another great concern was leaving her parents and children, she wondered that if something serious were to happen to them, such as an illness or accident, she wouldn't be able to arrive on time, the trip would take her at least one day.

The beautiful and sweet little princess Doménica

She felt prey to a boomerang of questions that went round and round in her head, invading her thoughts without letting her rest. On the other hand, she had to finish her university studies. She concentrated on them together with her thesis partner, Jaime Cornide, they worked every weekend, day and night, until finishing their thesis project and taking the final exam; they managed to achieve the academic postgraduate degree of Master's in Business Administration, MBA, while at the same time she continued to work intensely and getting rid of her house furniture and personal things. She had to leave everything, she couldn't take more than two suitcases, in addition to Terry's two; it caused her anxiety to get rid of some gifts and personal items, such as books and ornaments, belongings that had great sentimental value for her, others a symbolism, history and a feeling that united them with their origins and especially with the person who had given them to her. With her capacity for resilience, she concluded: material things are material things, the most beautiful and important things are the memories that I treasure in my heart.

She made the wedding preparations practically all by herself, from requesting an appointment at the civil registry for the marriage, looking for witnesses, making the guest list, to buying her wedding dress. And regarding her wedding dress, taking advantage of another trip to *Santiago* for work reasons, one of her cousins accompanied her to Casa de la Novia, a bridal shop, to choose and buy her dress. After reviewing several catalogues and magazines, she chose two wonderful models, having to return the next day to try them on. The saleswoman who attended them was very kind and commented in a questioning tone:

–Based on your facial features and your body, I will allow myself to choose and put aside other dresses that you can try on besides the two you have already chosen. Are you OK with that?

–Yes, of course, thank you very much, you are so kind.

When she returned the next day with her cousin, she tried on the first dress that she had chosen, it fit her very well; she loved the second dress as well, but the young lady who attended her brought over five more dresses that she could try on. They were really extraordinary, they looked like princess dresses, like something out of fairy tales. Esmeralda felt happy and enjoyed trying on the dresses and counting on the saleswoman's great help, who would fix her dress and even her hair to make her look much more beautiful. At that moment, it occurred to her that it would be a good idea to take a picture to have a more objective view and, she called her cousin over, who was sitting a few steps away, checking her cell phone.

–Cousin, please, can you take a picture of me, to see how the dress I like the most looks on me?

–Ah, yeah, wait a minute.

Without much enthusiasm she took two simple and plain pictures, without any special angles, even the saleswoman appeared in both photographs.

–Ah, yes it looks fine. Can you take a closer shot and another one with the other dress, please?

–But, why so many?

–I'm getting married and I want to buy the prettiest one, the one that fits the best.

–Yes, but it's not a big deal.

Esmeralda noticed that something strange was going on. She tried to avoid getting sad and continued trying on the other dresses, while her cousin continued to sit with her head down, bored and looking at her cell phone; the saleswoman offered to take pictures of her, which were amazing as if they had been taken by a professional photographer. Then, her cousin stood up saying that she wasn't feeling well and asked the saleswoman:

–By any chance, do you have some aspirin? I have a headache.

–No, I'm sorry, but there's a pharmacy round the corner.

Left alone, the saleswoman immediately approached Esmeralda commenting in astonishment and concern:

–Your cousin is terribly envious of you.

–What? Why do you say that?

–But if she even gets to vomit from how envious she is of you; you could totally tell by looking at her face, in the belittling way she looked at you, she even took the pictures reluctantly. That's why I preferred taking them.

–No, I don't think so; my cousin even brought me here in her car.

–Take a good look, look at that other bride, see how her mother and friends help her with the dresses; they are happy, radiating joy, they look very content, they are having a great time and, your cousin, just lying there on the couch. Be careful with her, remember that envy is one of the seven capital sins; she can cause you a lot of harm.

Esmeralda appreciated her comments and warnings, but she just couldn't believe it, although it generated certain degree of concern.

Between the wedding preparations and the requirements of the Chilean civil marriage law, it was contemplated to have two witnesses for the bride and two for the groom as well, so Terry travelled joined by two of his closest friends, Andrew and David, who attested that he was divorced and had no impediment to marry.

Esmeralda stopped by the *Hotel Rocas de Bahía Inglesa* on two occasions, to make sure that everything was fine with her wedding night reservation and that the jacuzzi was functioning. Even the day Terry arrived in Chile, three days before the wedding, taking advantage of the fact that they were going to have lunch at the hotel restaurant, together they reconfirmed the reservation. Esmeralda wanted to make sure that everything was impeccable, especially that when arriving to the hotel, the room was tempered, because since it was winter time, it was very cold and even more so bearing in mind that at night, in the desert, the temperatures usually dropped to minus zero degrees. Once again, they confirmed that everything was fine, that there was nothing to worry about.

There were only three weeks left until the celebration of her marriage, Esmeralda continued working intensely, trying to do as many post-sale services as possible and carrying out work, in order to facilitate the induction process of her relief. That day being a very peculiar one and having her schedule full of activities in the field, she got up earlier than usual to arrive at the mining camp to give the induction speech to the workers, before they started their work day, since the company was located more than two hundred kilometres away from her home.

She was ending a very intense day; she was exhausted and eager to get home as soon as possible to rest. On the way back to Copiapó, she was driving very alert and holding tightly to the steering wheel of her vehicle. Facing the irregularities of the mining roads, it was very dangerous to drive; also because of how curvy they were, making visibility difficult. It required great ability to drive, which she had thanks to the experience and skills acquired during her years as a raider being a member of the Copiapó 4 x 4 Raiders Club, where she was baptized and became known as "The Muse of the Atacama Desert". They were years of practicing adventure sports in which she experienced high adrenaline at a thousand per hour, manoeuvring and managing on her motorcycle and on her jeep to go up and down the *Mar de Dunas* and *Duna Madre*, her fascination being going down to the Embudo Chico, just as she enjoyed with admiration seeing her most daring companions with more powerful machines, such as Patricio Ríos, El Regalón, Magila, Pipo Zaro, Ivo Danianich, among many others, who excelled doing tricks in the Big Funnel. Esmeralda, with her mischievous and playful girl's soul, loved to ride from wall to wall as fast as she could on her motorcycle, *El Tobogan* (the Slide), of more than three hundred meters long in the shape of a true serpentine. Close to reaching the main road and driving in those adverse conditions, with the adrenaline and stress at full blast, she was worried because her phone wouldn't stop ringing. When she reached a plain, she stopped and saw three missed calls from Renata; she immediately returned the call and her daughter responded very agitated and with a worried voice:

–Mum, mum, Apollo is sick, he's been hospitalized since yesterday because he has fallen ill, he's having issues with his stomach and apparently, they are going to operate him, we are not sure yet, they have him in observation, everything depends on how he gets through the night and wakes up tomorrow.

Renata spoke fast, she was known for speaking in an accelerated way, but with her nerves she did it even faster, while her mother listened, trying to assimilate the serious news she had been told.

–Oh, no, no! It can't be, I hope to God it's only a simple stomach ache, something that gave him an upset stomach. What did he eat? Tell me!

–On Saturday we went out for Chinese food, at the corner restaurant and, since the plates were really big, we brought the leftovers home; it was Mongolian meat with chao fan rice. It was really tasty and yesterday on Sunday, Apollo ate everything without heating it up.

–Ah, you see! That's probably what caused it, it'll go away soon –Esmeralda commented with a tone of relief.

–Hopefully it's that and nothing more serious, mum.

–They have him with an IV bag, right?

–Yes, he has an IV bag, but he's complaining that he's in a lot of pain, that he's bloated, has stomach cramps and that he can't go to bathroom.

–My poor baby. Please, let me know if anything happens, I'm on the road but as soon as I get home, I'll call you back. I'll be very attentive to the phone.

When she arrived home, Renata told her that Apollo was still the same, that everything would be decided tomorrow. Esmeralda informed her boss that her son was in poor health and that she would probably have to travel to *Santiago.* And so, it was. The next day, Renata called her mid-morning, confirming that yes, they were indeed going to perform surgery and, that they had already taken him to the ward. Esmeralda, who was going up to a mining site, asked her colleague and friend Marsella, to please turn back around to return to Copiapó, because she had to urgently travel to Santiago*,* since they were going to operate on her son, that everything had to be suspended, and to please take her to the airport. Upon arrival, she ran up to the front desk requesting to buy an emergency ticket to Santiago on the next flight, they replied that there was no ticket available for the next flight, but that there was room on the evening one. She tirelessly insisted if they could please make an exception and let her get on the next flight, explaining that she needed to travel urgently, that her son's life was at risk of death, to which they replied:

–I'm sorry, madam, the flight is completely full, there are no available seats, but if a passenger cancels their flight or doesn't arrive on time, I can give you their place, although there are other passengers who are also waiting to fly and have priority before you.

The wait was endless, stressful and exhausting; at the same time, she had to make great efforts to stay put together and calm, in order to communicate with her boss and her clients, to inform them that she wouldn't be able to fulfil the commitments agreed for that day and the days following, due to her son's serious health condition. At that moment, a man approached her, who very kindly offered to give her his ticket for the next flight to Santiago, commenting that he could take the evening flight because he was in no rush to arrive early to the capital. Esmeralda thanked him with all her heart and together they went to the front desk to inform the airline official about the agreement they had made. To their amazement and irritation, they received an unexpected and rude reply:

–I'm sorry, you can't exchange flight tickets and, you, madam, stop making a scandal and bothering our passengers.

The man, with a soul of a good Samaritan, replied with a firm tone and maintaining his calm:

–Please, madam, give the lady my seat, I'll take the evening flight and insisted, raising his tone of voice and looking directly at her: Give the lady my seat, I'm in no rush to travel, I'm putting myself in her shoes with her son being seriously ill and I will happily give her my ticket.

At that point he was no longer calling her "madam", but instead they were referring to her as the rude and unconscious chick. at that moment, they made the boarding call and again Esmeralda, leaving her pride and shame aside, approached the lady begging to be allowed to make use of the other man's ticket; the employee responded in a bad way, although giving her very good news:

–Both of you can board, because some tickets were freed.

–Thank you, Lord! –she exclaimed as her new little angel looked at her smiling and giving a deep sigh of relief, her soul returned to her body and, they both embarked very happy, although obviously she was devastated and extremely worried about her son Apollo. She got on the plane but not before infinitely thanking her new Samaritan friend for the gesture of great generosity. The man pointed out that she had nothing to thank him for, and offered, upon arriving in Santiago, to take her in his personal vehicle to the clinic where her son was, since he was getting picked up at the airport. Upon arriving at the clinic, she got out running to find Renata and her ex-husband in the waiting room, accompanied by some of his relatives, Esmeralda's ex-sisters-in-law and nieces, and also Mario's new girlfriend, with the luck that in that precise moment the physician approached them to inform them about Apollo's surgery, addressing Mario and his sisters. Esmeralda, drawing strength from weakness, interrupted the doctor:

–Excuse me, doctor, I'm Apollo's mother, I've just arrived from Copiapó, I was at work, please, tell me how my son is doing.

The surgeon greeted her and continued giving the update on Apollo's state of health and how complicated the surgery had been, directing his gaze now at Esmeralda:

–It was a very complex surgical intervention, lasting more than six hours because the medical team faced an infinity amount of adhesions, making it difficult to access and visualize the intestine in its entirety, in search of any possible obstruction and bending. Fortunately, we didn't find anything –adding–, however, the intervention was absolutely necessary, to check and rule out any possible obstruction, because otherwise, if there had been one, it could have generated septicaemia.

–Doctor, but how is my son doing?

–He's stable, in the recovery room, waking up from the anesthesia.

–Doctor, please, can I see him?

–Yes, but only for a couple of minutes, you and the father, no one else, I'm sorry.

It was another very complex event in Esmeralda's life, because her children's lives were sacred to her, she was absent for two weeks from her work, dedicating herself exclusively to the care of Apollo, she was attentive to any unforeseen event, she spoke daily with the specialist medical team that attended him; his recovery was very slow, but he was progressing well. After several days of being hospitalized and under observation, he presented the first signs that his intestine was returning to normal: his first farts were the most anticipated farts and applauded by the medical staff, Apollo and his entire family; Esmeralda cried with emotion thanking God. Gone was the great scare that he had put them through. Once other complications in Apollo's digestive system were completely ruled out, via elaborate and rigorous examinations, scans and MRI's, Esmeralda prepared to return to Copiapó, saying goodbye to Apollo with deep pain, deeply lamenting that she wouldn't be able to accompany him until the day of his discharge. She was invaded by deep remorse of conscience and guilt knowing that she was going to get married while her son was hospitalized, she would never forgive herself, she knew that once she arrived in Copiapó, she would inevitably resume the plans for the marriage celebration, plans that remained unalterable, they would be carried out as organized; since there were countless circumstances, it was almost impossible to postpone the wedding date, especially considering the one hundred and fifty guests, who had bought their tickets with great anticipation and had arranged to join her on her momentous event. And without considering the large expenses she had made and the infinity of commitments assumed, she couldn't back out.

Her friends had prepared an entertaining bachelorette party for her at Marinela's house, who was the hostess along with her daughter Carlita, they also and generously accommodated in their home Terry's friends who had travelled expressly from London to be part of their friend's great happiness, and to be, the witnesses of the wedding and to take advantage of the opportunity to tour a large part of Chile; so, they extended their trip for three weeks. They were amazed with the natural tourist beauties, the climate, the gastronomy and its people.

In the behind-the-scenes of the preparations for the bachelorette party, there was a very funny anecdote: it turns out that Marinela wrote to the representative of the Tunas of the UDA (a group of students from the University of Atacama that perform concerts) to hire them and animate the party, who responded that he was sorry, that they didn't have time because the young musicians were in the middle of the exam period. The next day, she met by chance one of the young *tunos*, they greeted each other and she told him what a pity it was that they couldn't hire them and, he responded with a voice of regret:

–I'm sorry, it's just that we are super occupied studying, because it is the exam period.

–Yes, I know, what a pity, that's exactly what your director said and the saddest part is that the bride was so happy knowing that the *tunas* were going to be present for her bachelorette party and also, since she's moving to London, it would have been wonderful for her to take that memory of Las Tunas or of the music from "Los del Chañar" group.

–Ah!!! What! It's a bachelorette party? Wow! Why didn't you say that before? Of course, we can go and play!

–But how? What will happen with your studies and exams?

–Ah!! Don't worry about that! We'll manage somehow, tell me...tell me...tell me...when, where and at what time, and we'll be there, we won't fail you I promise, a *tuno's* word.

And so it was, the *tunos* all arrived at the party and, there were more *tunos* than those invited to the party. They had a great time, they had a lot of fun singing and dancing, making jokes, and Carlita's great idea to have a competition to see who could make a wedding dress, providing only toilet paper and greaseproof paper, as well as scissors and pins which resulted into two marvellous dresses like the ones designed and made by the great Versace.

Terry, meanwhile, had a bachelor party organized by his friends in London, who invited him to a rock concert by one of his favourite bands and then went to a few bars losing track of what they had drunk and not knowing how they had gotten home. They only remembered clearly what had scared off the drunkenness: it was running into Terry's ex-wife in the same carriage of the train wagon on the way home, unable to interpret whether it had been some omen, becoming an almost unusual and very mysterious event.

The wedding party was wondrous

The marriage was extraordinary; everything had been prepared with great taste, finesse and elegance. Her friend Verónica had done an amazing job decorating and organizing the venue, considering every detail, from the entrance with guards and guides to the parking lot for the vehicles, to the wonderful and romantic flower arch where the civil marriage ceremony would take place, with the participation of witnesses. The room gleamed with the flower arrangements and delicate candles on the tables, the light displays, the stage for the orchestra and the musicians, the huge, beautiful and tempting wedding cake, a dessert buffet and the open bar, that invited even the insulin-dependent and those on a diet. The civil ceremony was organized in the garden by the pool, under the arch of natural flowers, with chairs covered by fine silk lace and the pool filled with balloons and floating candles, decorations that her dear friend Marcia had given her. Everything was wonderful, ready, the majority of the guests had already arrived and, the groom was biting his fingernails in anticipation of his beloved Esmeralda, who was half an hour late for her arrival.

The bride looked stunning, dazzling with such beauty and majesty, her dress was precious with fine lace, delicate sequins around the neckline and on the chest, adjusted to the waist and wide from the hips, extending in a five meter long train that highlighted her delicate, fine and beautiful silhouette, her wavy black hair shined with the lights and the moonlight, filling the place with her presence and exquisite fragrance, causing admiration and happiness from her family and guests. She walked upright and smiling holding her brother Jaime's arm and not her father's, who was in poor health, he had made a great effort to participate in the marriage of his beloved daughter Esmeralda; he looked at her with great pride, tears in his eyes, together with his wife, who held him firmly by the arm, invaded by mixed feelings. They were very happy and excited about their daughter's happiness, but they were saddened and anguished by the fact that she was going to live so far away.

The stunning and radiant bride

The wedding party was tremendous, Esmeralda looked divine, radiant and extremely happy, it could have been a perfect celebration if it hadn't been for the sadness of not having the presence of Apollo, who was still hospitalized, and Renata, who hadn't arrived on time to the airport, because she had missed her flight; the rest was all wonderful, there were more than one hundred and fifty guests, among her friends and family and, her little grandchildren Viccencito and Doménica, who played a very important role in the wedding celebration, both dressed all in white, like their grandmother, looking very beautiful, awakening the admiration and emotion of those present, especially their grandmother, who couldn't avoid a couple of tears escaping. They threw flower petals from the entrance to the majestic arch where their grandmother had to walk; Viccencito was also responsible for passing the rings to the bride and groom, held together by a pair of silk ties in a beautiful and delicate satin and lace heart made by her friend Eloísa.

Cocktails were served on the terrace and in the gardens by the pool, the guests delighting in fine and exquisite delicacies while savouring a sparkling glass of champagne; dinner and the dessert buffet was also very tasty. The bride and groom's show was really beautiful, very romantic, dancing and performing a little piece of the love songs that united them, being a great surprise when they did the Chilean national dance, the *cueca*. Esmeralda managed to convince Terry to do the show and dance the *cueca* to *"La Consentida"*, which was her favourite *cueca*. The issue was that even though he had seen the *cueca* dance and several videos to familiarize himself with the dance, so that it would be easier for him to learn when Esmeralda taught him, between all the hustle and bustle and preparations for the wedding and the trip to England, they both had completely forgotten to rehearse. So, the night before the wedding, the hotel where they were staying had given them a night consisting of a dinner, in addition to decorating their room with red rose petals and giving them a bottle of champagne, and a silver tray with cheese, grapes and chocolates; they enjoyed such a well-deserved gift and the attention of the hotel and, being ready to go to sleep, Esmeralda reacted, quickly getting out of bed, still panting, perspiring and naked, saying with despair and concern to Terry:

–My love, my love, we need to practice the *cueca*.

And he began to search for the song *"La Consentida"* on YouTube, improvising a pair of handkerchiefs with a rose and a napkin, and completely naked, Terry learned to dance *cueca*, at least the basic steps, putting on a spectacular show at the wedding party, to such an extent that they gave him a standing ovation, especially for being a UK man and daring to dance the *cueca*, since the vast majority of Chileans, and especially men, don't know how or don't dare to dance it, they get very embarrassed, claiming that the choreography is too difficult, just because they don't want to make a fool of themselves. Even Víctor, a friend of Esmeralda's from the masters, gave him as a reward the poncho that he had lent him, so he could dress as a *huaso* when dancing the *cueca.* (A *huaso* is a Chilean man revered like a cowboy)

Terry dancing Cueca

Then they danced the bride and groom's waltz to the rhythm of live music performed by Cecilia, Esmeralda's cousin, who also masterfully interpreted the "*Ave María*" during her entrance to the venue; she had a spectacular soprano voice. There, the party went on until dawn, everyone happily danced and enjoyed themselves, the bride went around the entire dance floor with the groom, who were already husband and wife, dancing with each of the guests, Esmeralda with her male friends and, Terry trying to keep up with Esmeralda's rhythm, despite the fact that he always laughed and excused himself when they invited him to dance, saying that he couldn't dance because he had two left feet, that's what they say in England when a person doesn't have dancing skills, "I have two left feet." They all had a lot of fun with a mixture of English and Chilean traditions, like throwing the glove and the bouquet, taking off the bride's garter with their teeth, trying to match and make pairs, that's how her firefighter friend, Cristian El Peter, el Capo, together with his girlfriend, caught the bouquet and the glove, fulfilling in them the prophecy of marrying and, effectively the following year they were united in marriage.

Being around three in the morning, the couple began to say goodbye to the few guests who still remained at the party, to embark on a trip to Bahía Inglesa, forty-five minutes away from Copiapó, at which point Esmeralda realized that she had forgotten an important detail which was hiring a driver to drop them off at the hotel; a job that Terry had to take on. It was a very risky trip, they were both exhausted, they had drunk alcohol and were sleepy, it was a winter night and, in winter the darkness is more intense, added to the *camanchaca*, which wouldn't allow them to see beyond a couple of meters, forcing them to make a tremendous effort in staying awake. Fortunately, they managed to pass the stretch with *camanchaca* and continued the last kilometres without major inconveniences. When they got to the hotel, everything was dark, the lights were off and, the reception and the vehicle entrance gate with a key were both closed. They insistently honked the horn so someone could open the gate and, after five minutes, a man appeared with a flashlight, well clothed and even wearing a hat. Esmeralda annoyed and more than anything surprised, asked him to quickly open the gate so they could enter, and he strangely answered:

–But who are you?

–We have a reservation for the Premier Suite; let us through because it's cold out here.

–The problem is that all the rooms are occupied.

–But not ours, it's our wedding night –showing him that she was still in her wedding dress.

–I don't know, something must have happened because no one informed me of anything, let's go to the reception to see if they left me a note.

–He checked the entry book and the computer over and over again, moving his head and looking at the couple, he said:

–I'm sorry, like I said, all the rooms have been booked, even the Premier, which you say you reserved.

–Reserved? Paid for, I paid in advance for more security and we even came two days ago to check and the receptionist said that everything was ok with our reservation.

Without anywhere to stay, they called a couple of friends that had summer houses on the beach to ask them if they could spend the night in their homes, and everyone they called said the same thing:

–We would gladly give you the key, but unfortunately, we have them here in Copiapó.

It was a night of terror, they couldn't believe what they were living, it was already going to be six in the morning and-Esmeralda hugged her husband, bursting into tears, he also hugged her joining in on the crying. After eliminating some of the sadness and helplessness, Esmeralda looked him in the eye, apologizing for the hotel's irresponsibility and for not having a place to spend their wedding night. She felt very distressed and ashamed, because it was her country and having the certainty that something like this would never happen in England, which Terry had already repeated to her and to the hotel's night worker. Without having anywhere to sleep, they went for a walk along the beach shore, until they fell deeply asleep. They woke up after a couple of hours to the sun's rays and to the fluttering and shouting of seagulls. They headed to a public bathroom so Esmeralda could take off her wedding dress, which couldn't have been more battered after having dragged it across the floor when she took off her magical red high-heeled shoes at the party and then walking barefoot on the beach.

They met with their friends who had travelled from England and those who also came from other remote places in Chile, with whom they had arranged to have lunch on the beach; nobody could believe what they had experienced, lamenting the situation and not having been able to help them.

The plans to enjoy the weekend at the beach fell apart and they returned to Copiapó, to Esmeralda's house which was a mess, with boxes everywhere and so much clutter, devoting those couple of days to arranging everything to receive the tenants. Her daughter Victoria accompanied them to the airport and kept Esmeralda's car. They happily said goodbye, and she wished them a good trip and promised them a visit

The trip to London was exhausting, they felt it longer than it actually was, as a result of the accumulated fatigue and the tensions experienced, overcoming it with the wonderful memories of the wedding and having shared with their loved ones. It was a great relief to get off in São Paulo for the connecting flight, allowing them to walk around and stretch their legs when moving from one terminal to another to do the transfer.

Upon arriving at Heathrow airport in London, they separated to go through the immigration police, as Terry had a British citizen's passport and she didn't, having to stand in line for the non-European passengers. Already stepping on British soil, they both smiled feeling at home, in a couple of hours they would be able to finally shower and rest. However, Esmeralda was retained longer than usual by the immigration police, who asked her:

–Do you intend to stay and live in the United Kingdom?

To which she responded with absolute naturalness and joy:

–Yes, of course, because my husband is British, however, we're not sure, we're going to try it out for a while and if we don't get accustomed to it, we'll move back to Chile.

Faced with that answer, which was absolutely natural and true, the police officer asked her to take a seat and wait. Without asking any questions, she obeyed and patiently waited, until a female police officer arrived, asking her to accompany her, leading her to an office, where another apparently higher-ranking police officer was waiting joined by an interpreter, who asked her the same questions and more specific ones as well, about how they had met, how long it had been, in addition to asking about her visa to enter the United Kingdom. She answered:

–Yes, I have a visa; Chileans have tourist visas allowing them to stay in England for up to six months.

–However, you need a British spouse's visa.

–I am processing it, I did the processing online; it will take approximately three months for it to arrive.

–I'm sorry, but we can't let you enter the United Kingdom without a visa.

In that precise moment, Esmeralda realized that there was a problem, she replied with concern and in a pleading tone:

–Please, let me enter, I've just gotten married and I have a tourist visa.

–No, that visa doesn't work for you, besides you and your husband should know that the British spouse's visa is essential for entering; it's a fundamental requirement, without it you cannot enter.

Esmeralda broke down in tears, begging to be allowed in, insisting that she had a tourist visa for six months and that the other visa would arrive within three months. The chief police officer stood up and left the office, while the female police officer tried to calm Esmeralda and asked her to accompany her to another police waiting room, where there were three more people looking bored, tired and worried. The police told her to wait, that they were going to see on which flight they would send her back to Chile.

–What? No, no! I can't go back to Chile, I'm married and my husband is here in the airport waiting for me, I want to see my husband.

Esmeralda was devastated, she cried and screamed, pleading and imploring, she couldn't take it anymore. They allowed her to see Terry for only five minutes, who they had also interviewed separately and had checked both interviews. As soon as she saw him, she ran clinging to him with all her might, begging him to do something, that they couldn't deport her to Chile, that she loved him and that her new home and life was together with him there in England; to which he replied:

–Yes, my love, but there's nothing we can do, the police is extremely rigorous and we must respect everything they say and, if we have to process your visa... –she interrupted him reacting as if she had found the answer:

–Please, call the Chilean embassy in London, they know me, yes, they can help me.

–I've already called, it's closed and they gave me an appointment for tomorrow at nine in the morning.

–Tomorrow? No, no, it has to be now, I can't accept to be sent back to Chile, my life is here with you, not in Chile!

One of the police officers approached, showing Terry his watch and indicating that he had to leave. Esmeralda hugged him once more, holding on to him with all her might begging while sobbing for him not to leave, not to leave her alone.

The hours passed and it got dark, they brought a box with snacks made up of sandwiches, fruits and water. The police informed her that they were arranging for her return for the next day and she responded:

–No, because my husband is going to the Chilean embassy in London and they're going to help me.

–Good luck.

Esmeralda remembered that she was asthmatic and, if she got cold she could decompensate and suffer an asthma attack, and in those circumstances they wouldn't be able to send her back. So she went to the bathroom, got her hair and clothes as wet as possible, filled her boots with water and sat on the cold bathroom floor. After about twenty minutes, they knocked on the door, it was the police ordering her to leave the bathroom, surprised to see her soaked and asked her what had happened.

–Nothing –she responded sharply and with a furious face.

The police made her come out of the bathroom and locked the door, walking away and returning with a blanket, asking her to bundle up. Esmeralda cried inconsolably lying on the floor; feeling so cold she remembered Ananda and Brigu's yoga classes, and began to do the sun salutation pose, an exercise that demanded a lot of mobility. She quickly became energized and sat down to rest. A little sleepy, she went to the bathroom and got herself wet again, the police called her attention saying that she wasn't allowed to go back to the bathroom anymore.

Something super strange happened, despite the cold and having her clothes soaked in water on her body, she didn't present any signs or symptoms of a cold and even less of an asthmatic attack.

Around noon, Terry called her giving her the bad news that the consulate wasn't going to be able to do anything to help her; she had to comply with what the immigration police had told her to do. Feeling lost and having three police officers approach her to take her to board, she threw herself on the floor throwing a temper tantrum, screaming, crying and begging to be allowed to be with her husband, that she wasn't going to return to Chile; between three policemen they tried to hold her to take her to board, and one of them reacted saying:

–We can't take her on board the plane in this state.

Esmeralda hearing and realizing that her strategy was working continued screaming and kicking harder. The policemen released her and she went to sit down. She was transferred to a temporary detention centre, where they took her fingerprints, front and profile photographs and they hung a card around her neck with her picture and a number. She had entered a detention centre; then after passing the identification and registration process, she was taken to a room where they ordered her to remove all her clothes and take a shower, they passed her a gown and pants and indicated the room where she would sleep in; there were many women, apparently of different nationalities due to their physical appearance.

Esmeralda made use of the computer that they kindly lent her to communicate with her family, where she spent hours and hours; the place was very clean, comfortable and they treated her kindly. She received care from a psychologist, who very gently explained the police procedures, making interventions and explaining that she had to return to Chile, process her visa and return. The policewoman, who had accompanied her from the counter to enter England and to the office where she had been interviewed by her boss, was working in the detention area; she sympathized with her and sat down to speak with her. Esmeralda told her how sad she was, and talked as if they were friends, placing her trust in her. The policewoman's name was Sarah, and she visited her several times a day, just like the psychologist. Together they managed to appease and convince

Esmeralda to return to Chile to process the visa that would allow her to enter the United Kingdom.

Esmeralda didn't trust that she would be allowed to enter on a second opportunity, the police assured her and told her about similar cases of other passengers and how they had entered when they returned with their visas in order. Sarah gave Esmeralda her phone number and her email so that she could call and write to her in case of any questions, as well as to let her know when she returns to be attentive to her arrival and to support her in whatever way was necessary. On the third day of staying in the police detention centre, Sarah informed her that they would come for her to take her to board that day. Esmeralda burst into tears once again, clinging on to the police, who by then treated her as if she were her daughter. They gave her the opportunity to see her husband, with whom she planned how to obtain the visa, that as soon as she arrived in Chile, she would go to the British embassy in Santiago and urgently request the processing of her visa. Terry took the four suitcases and the sewing machine home, traveling alone with her backpack. They said goodbye with deep sadness; they were devastated, destroyed and frustrated for not being able to prevent her from being deported. On the way to the plane, she was accompanied by Sarah and two male police officers. Upon reaching the boarding area, Esmeralda panicked and demanded that Sarah talked with the person in charge of the airport, with the chief police officer, the highest ranking police officer, she replied that it would be impossible.

–I'm not leaving without talking to him; I need him to promise that when I return, he'll allow me in.

They granted her the request to prevent her from having another tantrum and not wanting to board the plane. They took her to the same office where she had previously been, they made her sit and wait for the chief police officer. A very tall policeman entered, with an angry face and a shirt full of medals, accompanied by an interpreter; the interview was very short and took place in a tense environment. Esmeralda addressed him with a very serious tone:

–I need you to assure me that when I return to London with my visa, I won't have any problems entering.

–If you bring the correct visa and your passport, you will not have any issues entering.

–But I need to be certain of that.

–You have my word.

–I need your name.

He wrote it down on a sheet of paper that was on his desk, passed it to her and left very angrily. Esmeralda managed to read and verify the name on the plaque and see the identification number, which she wrote next to his name.

The policemen accompanied her to the plane and Sarah said goodbye very affectionately and compassionately. And so, Esmeralda undertook the return to Chile, after having been deported.

Visa denial and… deportation back to Chile

CHAPTER VII

The Pilgrim Bride in search of happiness

Exhausted, shattered and absolutely destroyed, they took her back to Santiago, Chile, with her marvellous and magical little red shoes, with the firm conviction and purpose of processing her visa as a matter of urgency and returning as soon as possible to meet again with her beloved Terry. Determined to achieve her goal, she immediately went to the British Embassy located in Las Condes, Santiago, and took a taxi in order to optimize time. At the reception office of the diplomatic building, she made her situation known, receiving the reply that she had to arrange a hearing and that the closest available time would be in twenty days, to which she replied that she couldn't wait, that she needed her visa immediately. She insisted, letting it be known that it was an urgent matter and, they answered her that, if her situation was so particular and urgent, that it would be best to travel and process the visa in Rio de Janeiro. The official who attended her told her that visas were not processed in Santiago but in Brazil, since it was a private company that issued the visas, adding that if she travelled, she could manage it faster.

She appreciated the suggestion and bought a ticket to Brazil for Monday, leaving the weekend free to go to the countryside to visit her parents, who were extremely concerned about the situation she was experiencing. On Monday, as soon as she arrived in Brazil, she immediately went to the British Embassy located in Botafogo, and to Esmeralda's regret it was closed. The security guard suggested that she go to the Chilean Consulate to request help, which was also closed, as it was almost five in the afternoon. They replied through the interphone saying to come back the next day, at ten o'clock in the morning, but at that point the tension and frustration was so great that she couldn't take it anymore and broke down in tears, begging to be attended to, that she didn't know what to do and had nowhere to go.

In response, a very kind lady came down, who happened to be the consul's secretary. She explained to her in great detail the deportation she had gone through and the urgency of obtaining a visa to return to England and reunite with her husband. The consular official, sympathetic to Esmeralda, made a grand exception: she allowed her to enter the consulate.

They both went up in an old elevator with accordion-type iron bars, which made some noise when opening and closing; they went up to the sixth floor and walked up a wide marble staircase until they reached the seventh floor, where they were attended by an elderly lady, who looked right for job. That lady, however, was grumpy about having to attend to Esmeralda, despite the fact that the consulate was closed. But she helped her to Google the required form to apply for the visa, although it was a great challenge as the page was in English; between the two of them, with a not so great command of the British language, they filled it out, but there were an infinity of questions to answer because it was information referring to Terry. They agreed to finish the process the next day, once Esmeralda obtained the missing data.

The lady kindly said goodbye and recommended that she stay at a nearby hotel, where Chilean delegations usually stayed at. With incredible solicitude, the consul's secretary coordinated with the hotel and offered to take her there, but before, she gave her a tour of some of the diplomatic premises, clarifying that she could come when she wanted and needed, during office hours, of course and, that she could use the internet and the kitchen, and even showed her a huge bathroom with a shower and a laundry room, adding that she could also use them whenever she needed.

Esmeralda responded:

–Thank you very much, but don't worry, I won't be needing them since I'll only be in Brazil for a couple of days, returning then to Chile and, from there flying back to England –she showed her the backpack, adding that she hadn't even taken a suitcase, she was only travelling with her laptop, some medicine and a change of clothes. The secretary smilingly replied:

–One never knows, we only know when we'll arrive but never when we'll leave, sometimes the paperwork takes a little longer than expected. Hopefully it's not your case.

–No, it won't be my case, don't worry, thank you anyway – Esmeralda said calmly while she laughed in silence, thinking about her marvellous and magical little red shoes that would take her back to England as soon as possible, just like they had taken her to the most extraordinary places in the world, which she had never dreamed of seeing, just like when she had been invited to spend Christmas in Egypt when she was supposed to be in London, while she was studying English and the school had closed for the end of the year holidays. She threw her magical little red shoes into the air and they fell nothing more and nothing less than in Egypt, in the land of Tutankhamen. She often asked herself "how not to love my magical little red shoes, so envied and coveted by my friends? People have even had the audacity to ask to borrow them from me, but it's impossible, I'm sorry, their magic only works on me."

The Alcázar hotel was ten blocks from the consulate and between them was the British Embassy. She requested a single room which was very comfortable; it had cable TV, telephone and breakfast service. She called Terry, told him everything she had done and asked him for the information she needed, after which she felt it was time to rest and relax. She took a nice bath when she was tempted by the aromatic bath salts that she had at her disposal, ordered room service and ended that long and exhausting day watching a romantic love movie, although after a few minutes she fell asleep.

The next morning, she returned to the consulate to finish the visa application form and went to deliver it to the company that carried out those procedures, there they told her that she had to attach other documents and take them in a sealed envelope. Esmeralda commented that she was in a hurry to return to England and asked, if they could please make an exception for her and give her priority, their response was:

–The faster you come back and present your application, the faster you'll obtain your visa.

And so she did, she returned in the course of the afternoon and after delivering the documents they informed her that she would have to wait three weeks; God! She replied that she couldn't wait, and insisted that they please make an exception, but it was impossible.

Resigned to waiting, she devoted herself to sightseeing; she toured Botafogo, Ipanema and Copacabana, the beaches being her fascination and relaxation, she visited museums and tourist attractions, and thus the first week peacefully passed by. From the second week on, she began to miss Terry more every day and the days became endless. When the three weeks were up, they called her from the consulate telling her that the envelope she was expecting had arrived.

Esmeralda jumped with joy and ran to the consulate to find the envelope containing her passport and visa. But, surprise! They told her that she had failed to attach a certificate proving her level of English, as well as other documents related to her husband that she hadn't presented due to ignorance and her precarious command of the language. She felt faint once again, helpless and frustrated, it was too much for her to handle on her own. She felt overwhelmed and, despite the great support she received from the consulate and hotel staff, she cried nonstop; it was one of those days when she wished she hadn't existed. Everyone around her regretted her situation and felt sorry for Esmeralda as they saw her sadder and more upset as the days went by, thinning and withering like a flower without water. The story of the pilgrim bride had begun.

The financial aspect was another issue that she had to deal with, the wedding expenses had been large, they had used up all their savings, and when she found herself in another country, without work and without income, the situation was difficult for her, in addition to having to pay the visa taxes and the related procedures, which were of a large amount. Apart from that, she also had to pay for the right to take the English test that was required of her as part of the innumerable documents for the process of obtaining her visa. The closest date for the exams was in a month, and with deadlines and more deadlines, the wait seemed eternal.

The stress began to generate tension in the newlywed's relationship and the first discussions arose. Esmeralda reproached Terry for the fact that he hadn't been involved from the beginning in the visa procedures, realizing that most of the documents and information required were related to him and not to her, and reminded him of what the immigration police at Heathrow airport had said, that they should have known that a marriage visa was required to enter the UK, that it was impossible that he, being British, hadn't known that, but Terry was completely unaware and, so was she.

Faced with the financial pressure, she was forced to administer austerely the little money she had left, reducing her expenses as much as possible, changing to a simpler room, eating only breakfast and, being that her only chance to eat, she had to eat as much as she could. She would prepare a couple of sandwiches and take fruits to pass the day, getting up early and going to the consulate to spend the whole day studying English for the exam; there she would connect to the internet for free and thus avoid paying for said service at the hotel. She also began using the consulate's kitchen and laundry room, which she never thought she would do. Every afternoon she would arrive very tired at the hotel; it was a working day without working but concentrating on studying. She would leave her books and laptop and go for a walk, day after day, pilgrimage through the streets, being able to remember by heart what was in every nook and cranny of the path going and returning from the beach, going back to the hotel to continue studying and practicing English tests, after which she would fall into bed exhausted by the fatigue and accumulated stress. It was during that time, that she contacted her friend Luzia through Facebook, who invited her to her home in Victoria so that she could relax and prepare herself more calmly for the English test. Esmeralda accepted the invitation, she felt it was a great opportunity to regain energy and relax, to be able to share with her friend, eat well, get to know and find herself in an environment of relaxation and comfort to continue studying.

Luzia's family was very large and cramped, she remembered going with her twice to one of her older sister's house, where they were preparing her parents' wedding anniversary celebration; they enjoyed and suffered watching Brazil play against Chile in the 2014 World Cup qualifiers match, both wore their football jerseys from their respective countries celebrating Brazil's triumph with a good glass of champagne, with the regret of Esmeralda, who would have preferred her *La Roja de Todos' (*Chile national football team)to win.

Upon her return to Botafogo, she requested to move to another smaller room, as her critical financial situation was increasing. She rented a small room in the upper part of the hotel, where the service rooms were located, devoid of comforts and having to share the bathroom with the other guests on that floor.

Finally, the date of the English test arrived; she turned it in and obtained the minimum score required to process the visa, she applied for it again for the third time, and there, yes, she met absolutely all the requirements and once again had the support of the consulate, having to wait the unavoidable three weeks to receive the visa and, that was time to relax and unwind.

She made an exception and went to celebrate in Ipanema, got on a public transport bus, walked along Avenida del Mar with her magical little red shoes and then took them off to walk along the shoreline, playing with the waves that lapped over her feet. It was something that fascinated her. She also took photographs and would ask tourists to take some of her. For dinner, she chose a restaurant on the beach shore, which caught her attention and attracted her due to its strategic location among palm trees and for entertaining tourists and customers with live music. She ordered an exquisite common sole with a side of salad and a glass of Chilean wine, ending it with an order of ice cream with fruit and, serving herself two glasses of whisky with ice while enjoying the bossa nova and the song that the musicians dedicated to her, the famous "Girl from Ipanema". It was a divine night despite being alone, that for her wasn't an issue. In her years as a divorced woman, she had learned to enjoy her own company and, better yet, she loved to travel alone on holidays abroad.

When it was time to pay the bill, her credit cards were rejected by the system, they tried on several occasions, but they couldn't carry out the transaction; the waiter gave her the option of paying in cash, but it was impossible because she didn't have any money on her. He suggested that she go to the hotel to get the other card, but it was night time and the hotel was half an hour away. Esmeralda, very embarrassed by the stifling situation, offered to leave her jewels, watch and camera, as security and return the next day to settle the bill, although it hadn't been necessary. She said goodbye with the conviction that she would return first thing in the morning to pay for dinner, but unfortunately her cards had been blocked; the bank informed her that it would take 48 hours to reactivate them. She had to turn to Terry to send her money, and after three days, she was only able to return to Ipanema. As she approached the restaurant, the waiter recognized her, approached her almost running, raised his arms to the sky, thanking her and exclaimed:

–I thought that maybe you had returned to your country and I was going to have to pay for you bill.

–No, never! I took long because I had to solve the problem with my credit cards.

They hugged each other as if they were great friends, he breathing relieved and she grateful for the trust he had given her. She took the opportunity of ordering herself a Cuban mojito and relax while enjoying the music and the ocean breeze that caressed her skin and played with her hair.

When she arrived at the hotel, they gave her a message, it was from her daughter Renata, who had called her with the news that her graduation ceremony was coming up. Obviously, Esmeralda wanted to be there for her daughter during that important step in her life where she would be obtaining the degree of dental surgeon. After ensuring that her passport with her visa was being sent to Chile, she crossed the Andes Mountains using a special pass. She stayed at her aunt Carmencita's house, who had always welcomed her into her home with great affection and generosity, even more so now in the very adverse circumstances in which she found herself. Her aunt had been divorced for many years, one of her daughters lived at home, who was married and had two teenage children.

On the day of the graduation ceremony, Esmeralda arrived at the university an hour early, making sure to be on time and having a good place. Since she was the first person to arrive at the auditorium, she had the opportunity to meet and share with some of Renata's teachers and the privilege of choosing a seat in the first rows, reserving one for Apollo and another for her ex-husband, but they arrived half an hour late and weren't able to sit next to her. The ceremony was simple and passed very quickly and, at the end of the event they shared at a reception held by the university, leaving after to have lunch with Renata's closest friends. The conversation was pleasant and revolved around the studies Renata had carried out and the anecdotes she commented with her friends, without touching at all the difficult situation that Esmeralda was going through; in any case, she wasn't affected by it as she was aware of the coldness with which they used to treat her, and that the reunion was to celebrate the culmination of university studies and Renata's degree.

Renata's degree graduation

She remained in *Santiago* without moving, despite the fact that she eagerly wanted to travel to Copiapó to visit Victoria and to spoil her little grandchildren Viccencito and Doménica. She couldn't even wait at her parents' house in the countryside, which was less than two hours from Santiago because she had and wanted to be attentive to any unforeseen event that arose, such as the request for another document or some extra signature. Because of how long she stayed at her aunt Carmencita's house, things became tense, the atmosphere becoming rarefied as the days passed. It's known that for a visit to be pleasant, it shouldn't extend for more than a week; the fewer days, the better. In the case of Esmeralda, the situation was more complex, as it wasn't a visit per se, and without reasons or money to celebrate or share, she tried to accompany and help her aunt as much as she could and, mainly went out for walks aimlessly spending most of the days away from home, trying to avoid generating expenses and inconveniences.

Finally, and after the waiting period, she received the envelope that she had desperately wanted to be sent from Brazil: it was a large legal-size envelope containing her passport along with the form and documents she had presented and, a letter informing that her application, despite complying with all the required documentation and requirements, had been denied because it hadn't been processed from the country where she resided, meaning, from Chile. Absolutely devastated, she called Terry crying, telling him the terrible news and that she was giving up, that she was completely overcome by the situation that was impossible to continue. She felt that she was practically on the street, begging, without money, without work, without the comforts she was accustomed to having and, without her vehicle and her friends, whom she missed with her soul; they were her group of support, containment and joy.

Terry did everything possible to provide support and comfort over the phone, being practically impossible to do so; she was crying and crying for him to hug her, she needed to feel safe, protected and loved by him. Terry reacted with two great ideas, to travel to Chile to celebrate their honeymoon and to hire a lawyer to take over the visa procedures to avoid another rejection. He took the responsibility of coordinating with the lawyer and managing the visa, while travelling to Chile to enjoy a week-long honeymoon in Rio de Janeiro, where they visited the same places where Esmeralda had been. She revived, regaining hope and her smile. Together with Terry, she felt safe, happy and loved. Terry returned to London, managing to leave Esmeralda more calm and confident that everything would soon be a thing of the past.

During the honeymoon, in a conversation as a result of the impasses with the visa process and some decisions that hadn't been the most successful, Esmeralda took the opportunity to do what she called "clarity in the rules", leaving Terry perplexed. With a very soft and tender voice, she took him by the hands and, looking into his eyes, said:

–My love, I am a free woman and always will be, I love my freedom, my liberty is and always will be intractable.

Terry replied stuttering a bit and with an expression of not entirely understanding what Esmeralda was trying to say to him:

–I don't understand; what are you trying to tell me? –Adding–: No, no, you are not free! –taking her hand and showing her the wedding band on her finger–, we're married, you're my wife and you belong to me!

With the same sweetness but with firm temperance Esmeralda replied:

–My love, yes, of course we're married, I am your wife and I love you with all my heart, I am immensely happy with you, I enjoy with passion and intoxicating madness every night when we make love and, I wish that we are happy forever! However, I am not your property and you are not my property either, you and I are free and, we are together because we love each other and we decided to get married and share our lives. However, you have your own life made up of your two children, your parents, friends, rock, tennis, soccer, work, etc., in short, you have all your interests, hobbies and responsibilities that occupy and fill a large part of your life and your days; the same goes for me, I also have my own life which is made up of my great loved ones, being my grandchildren, my three children, my parents, family, friends, work, my interest in romantic, classical, and Celtic music and, my passion for opera, studying, volunteering, the Lions club, I love the ocean and gardening. And that life, my private life, is sacred and inalienable, but there is a third life, which is made up of you and I, it is a world of love and sharing as a couple, of joy and happiness, of sadness and problems, because without a doubt, there will be difficult moments that we will have to overcome together and in the best way possible with the least damage. Those are our three lives, my love.

–Ok, I understand and accept it, however, I also have my requirements and they're extremely important.

–Tell me!

–If one day you become interested in another person, please tell me right away, before entering in a more deep and sentimental relationship and, the same goes for me, if one day I become interested in another woman, I'll immediately let you know and in that precise moment our marriage will be over forever and we will get divorced.

–Deal. Let's make a toast to close our honourable pact, since it's already time for dinner.

During the time she stayed at her aunt Carmencita's house, two very significant events occurred in Esmeralda's life, not to mention that her cousin could no longer bear her presence in the house, making her life impossible and her aunt getting in the middle trying to calm the waters. Her other cousin asked her why she hadn't requested for a religious divorce, just like she had done. Esmeralda thought it was a good idea, she went to see the General Archbishopric of Chile in Santiago to request the Holy Church the annulment of her religious marriage, confident of the viability by keeping in mind that both her spiritual guide, the priest Rogelio of the Franciscan community, as well as the Bishop of Copiapó had mentioned this to her. After going through several interviews, they accepted the presentation of her request, the bishop personally interviewed the three witnesses that Esmeralda had presented, one of them was Elsita, what better testimony than her neighbour, who had seen her arrive in the town with nothing, starting her new life as a separated woman from scratch, using a drawer as a table and a jar of paint as a seat, cooking on a cooktop that she had generously provided, seeing how little by little and with much work she was putting together her little house. Elsita saw her and heard her cry when she wasn't able to see her children, after returning to her little house having walked for almost an hour there and another hour back, up the hill, out of breath, dusty and thirsty. She also listened when at midnight and early in the morning, her drunken ex-husband appeared, banging on the door and when she wouldn't open it, he becoming enraged shouting insults, kicking the door and stoning the roof of the house. Likewise, she saw her tears of sweat while carrying tons of rubble, dirt and stones, in order to lower costs, since the construction workers had left them on the front lawn, because the cleaning and removal service were not included in the installation of the gutter, repair and expansion of her house. Elsita was a great help during the months she was ill and, then when she returned from England, finding herself out of work. The process of annulment of her religious marriage would last approximately two years; she needed to have patience and faith that the Holy Pope would grant it.

The other event that happened, which was actually more of an embarrassing anecdote that Esmeralda had experienced, was that her dear friend Lissette seduced her into getting a beauty treatment with hyaluronic acid and Botox, with some doctors who were taking a training course and needed volunteer patients. Esmeralda, seeing that due to the many hardships she had endured, her face looked tired and deteriorated, agreed to be a volunteer. The doctors, happy with the patient, did everything for her, injected Botox and hyaluronic acid on her forehead, around the eye area and even around her lips to give her a little volume and shape. They told her that the treatment had been a bit invasive and that her face would look a bit red and swollen, and that the mouth area would be the most affected. Well, she exclaimed, don't worry, doctor, I am aware of that "to be a star you have to see stars."

When she got home, and like never before, as it was also a Saturday, the whole family was sitting at the table serving themselves *onces* (a Chilean snack), including Francisco and Gaspar, young teenagers who were rarely seen at home, and they invited her to join in. She only wanted to disappear from everyone's sight; she must have had an eyesore face, because everyone stared with an expression on their faces of exaggerated and irrepressible surprise and amazement. Aunt Carmencita asked her with a voice of astonishment and concern:

–Esmeraldita, for God's sake, what on earth happened to your lips that they're so swollen? –while her cousin asked with a tone and face of morbid curiosity:

–What have you done, have you gotten Botox?

–No, no, are you crazy, with what money, if I don't have money for anything –Esmeralda replied acting innocent while she tried to invent a good explanation for it.

–Yeah, but you had something done, it's impossible that you haven't had something done to your face looking red and swollen, your lips look like a blowfish's mouth –her cousin replied, causing everyone to laugh and, Esmeralda with the irresistible desire to leave, took a deep breath and responded in a soft and rueful voice:

–What happened was that Renata needed patients to practice dental moulds and prostheses, so she asked me if I could help her by being her patient and, of course I accepted She put some iron frames that bothered a lot and I had to open my mouth very wide, she also left them in for several minutes, until the cement dried; they were different moulds, it was terrible –adding in a questioning tone–: does my mouth look very swollen?

–Yes –Gaspar replied laughing–, just like a blowfish's mouth, like my mom said.

–Poor Esmi, honey, have some cold water, you could try doing compresses with a wet nap over your face and lips and, taking ibuprofen to lower the swelling, her aunt Carmencita replied, very concerned trying to help her and alleviate the discomfort, while her cousin made faces and growled without believing a single thing she was hearing.

It was a very embarrassing situation and, to this day, she couldn't understand why she hadn't explained what had really happened, probably so as not to be censured. As soon as she told Renata, she became furious as she felt that she was professionally discrediting her.

The long-awaited day finally arrived, they summoned her to the British Embassy in Santiago for the biometric examination, fingerprinting and signatures, an opportunity in which they analysed the reasons why her visa application had been rejected three times: the first evidently, was because it had been poorly formulated, the second time there were missing documents and the third time was due to a scoundrel from the visa processing company in Brazil, who, knowing that it had to be processed in the applicant's country of residency, received the application for the second time in order to keep the money for his services and visa taxes, which couldn't be returned in case of rejection. A senior diplomatic official explained it to her, who also apologized for the erroneous information they had given her at reception, suggesting that she travel to Brazil to expedite obtaining the visa, which was incorrect, making an exception with

Esmeralda, as a gesture of compensation for the damages caused, delivering the visa urgently in just three days. Esmeralda, elated with joy, called Terry giving him the great news; on this occasion, the tears shed were the product of extreme happiness and delirium that surrounded them, eager to embrace and start life together as they had decided and wished.

She travelled to Copiapó to say goodbye to Victoria, to enjoy her grandchildren and to reunite again and say goodbye to her friends. They were frantic days of overflowing joy, her magical little red shoes, infected with the adrenaline of their owner, took her from one place to another and, back in Santiago she withdrew the long-awaited visa to move to the United Kingdom, thanking God and the universe for the great favour granted after so much effort, tears and sacrifices.

Esmeralda left the trip to the countryside for last, saying goodbye to her parents, who once again blessed her and wished her the greatest happiness in the world, hoping to see her again at least once a year, to which she had already committed and would fulfil it, as well as at least a phone call a week.

She undertook the trip back to London, submerged in a boomerang of mixed feelings, she couldn't be happier, but the experience of the previous trip which had been so traumatic, made her feel insecure, although she had already communicated with Sarah, the police who had promised to help her and facilitate her entry. She wouldn't breathe easily until she passed the immigration police barrier and merged into the most wonderful love embrace with her beloved 21st century prince.

CHAPTER VIII

The reunion with her 21st century prince

As soon as Esmeralda received the long-awaited visa, she almost ran out of the British Embassy in *Santiago,* looking at the sky with teary eyes and with the passport in her hands; she raised her arms, her gaze fixed on an indeterminate point of infinite blue, and exclaimed:

–Thank you, thank you, thank you, God! I finally have my visa! Thank you, thank you, my beloved Jesus Christ, for everything, for your infinite love and mercy! I can finally travel to England and reunite with my beloved Terry!

Right after, she called him and with the same joy and emotion she thanked God, she said:

–My love, my love, I have the visa! Yes, they finally gave me the visa, I'm over the moon, I love you, I love you, I love you, I love you! How I wish to hug and kiss you, my love...! I miss you so much, I can't live without you; everything is terrible and harder without your presence!

–Wow, wow, finally! I'm so happy as well! –He responded, invaded by emotion and joy–. You have to travel immediately.

–Yes, yes, today I'm buying my ticket!

She left walking and jumping of joy through the beautiful streets of the investment and business centres of Las Condes. As soon as she got home, she shared the news with her beloved aunt Carmencita and the whole family, who were very happy and thanked God.

She only had three days, which had to be enough to travel to the countryside to say goodbye to her parents, and go north to enjoy with her beloved little grandchildren. They were days of intense emotion and joy, but as the date of her flight approached, the anguish and panic also increased of having to live the same situation once again and not being allowed to enter the country. Perhaps for most people it was a ridiculous or absurd fear, but for her it was terrible, the experience had been so painful that it would be very difficult to overcome.

She remembered putting in her handbag, along with the important documents, the identification card of the manager of Heathrow airport and Sarah's contact, the police who had accompanied her on to the plane and had supported her emotionally. In fact, she had communicated with her by emails, telling her that she already had her visa and the date of the trip. Sarah was very happy and asked for the itinerary and flight number to be attentive.

Esmeralda, with her facility to make new relationships, had created certain ties of friendship with the policewoman, with whom she exchanged emails from time to time commenting on the development of her visa process. Upon her arrival at the Barajas airport in Madrid, fear and anguish had taken hold of her, to the point that it was difficult for her to stand up and react to boarding calls to London, just by seeing and hearing the name. "Heathrow London airport", blocked and paralyzed her. She cried the entire flight to London, she prayed imploring God not to be deported again. When the plane landed, she was the last to get off, she could barely walk through the narrow, long and endless corridors of the airport, the queues at the immigration police were endless, it took her almost two hours to advance until she reached the counter and was attended. The officer, who was requesting the passports, responded to her greeting by asking the typical questions of rigour, where was she coming from, for how long and her intentions to stay and live.

–Mmm, please, you're going to have to take a seat and wait a few minutes.

–What? Why are you doing this to me, again? I have my visa, no, no, history cannot be repeating itself! –she screamed and sobbed.

A woman part of the staff, guided her to an area of the airport so she could sit and wait. As soon as she could, she called Terry to tell him what was going on with the immigrations police. She cried and cried inconsolably, unable to utter a single word...

–My love, please, calm down, what's wrong? Tell me!

–I'm a good person, honest, I'm not a delinquent –sobbing on the telephone.

–Surely there must be a misunderstanding, calm down, my love; I'll see what I can do.

–I don't want to be here, let's live in my country, yes, please, let's move to Chile, you'll be welcomed there, we'll look for jobs for you and we'll live in my house in Copiapó. And that way, we'll be closer to my little grandchildren, please, my love... –Esmeralda begged crying.

–Yes, my love, we'll do whatever you want, but, please, calm down, everything will be fine, I promise –Terry replied very apologetic, wishing that everything would be over once and for all, the wait was unbearably long, extremely painful and unfair for poor Esmeralda.

And then she saw Sarah approaching her at a firm pace, Esmeralda ran and hugged her, sobbing and imploring her help:

–Sarah, Sarah! Please, please, please, help me! Despite having the visa, I was told I had to get, they won't let me through! Why not? I don't understand!

–But who said that? No, no, Esmeralda, that's not right, you have your visa meaning you have the right to enter the United Kingdom! Please, stay calm, let me see what's going on!

–Yes, but your colleagues are retaining me here! Why, why?

–Please, calm down, I'm really sorry, Esmeralda, everything will be OK, I promise ––then she added in between mumbles and thinking out aloud, as she shook her head from side to side, grinning in disapproval and in extreme concern, I think it was an absolutely bad idea.

She turned to Esmeralda and with a voice of concern and compassion said:

–Esmeralda, I'm deeply sorry, this situation is absolutely unfair, please, calm down and come with me, follow me.

–Where are you taking me, where are we going? Please, please, Sarah... help me, you promised me, don't retain me here in the airport, I need to see my husband! –Esmeralda begged sobbing while strongly holding on to her with both hands and looking into her eyes; meanwhile Sarah, like her, couldn't bear it anymore, the situation had gotten out of hand and they needed to end it right then and there!

The policewoman had to make superhuman efforts not to reveal what was happening, she wanted to hug her and tell her everything once and for all. Looking into her eyes, with evident concern and sadness and very annoyed with herself, she realized that what they had planned hadn't been a good idea at all, she wanted to tell her, but couldn't, to the point that she had to bite her tongue on more than one occasion to keep quiet; she had to do so out of respect for her superiors. Responding to Esmeralda's pleading look, she took her by the hands and said with infinite sweetness:

–Dear Esmeralda, everything is OK, there's nothing to worry about, please, forgive my colleagues and forgive me, please, dry your tears and come with me to see my boss.

Esmeralda exclaimed euphorically:

–Is it the same police officer that I asked to promise me I'd be able to enter when I came back with the visa and, had said yes?

–Yes, that's exactly who we are going to see!

Esmeralda jumped with joy, her soul returned to her body and she trusted Sarah, obeying her like a child would to their mother. She took out a battered, wrinkled and wet handkerchief from one of her jacket pockets, wiped away her tears and after blowing her nose, walked behind the police, confident that everything would be resolved.

Great was her joy: upon entering the spacious and cold office she found herself face to face with the chief of police who had promised to allow her to enter England when she returned with a married woman's visa. Pouncing on the policeman, she screamed and pleaded:

–Mister Brian...! Please, please, let me enter, look, I have my visa here, I processed it, here it is, you promised that I'd be allowed to enter, please, please.

Sarah looked at her boss with deep concern, feeling responsible and guilty for what was happening. The policeman responded by frowning and shaking his head from side to side, just as she had done a few minutes ago with Esmeralda:

–Please, Esmeralda, can I see your passport? –while stretching his arm out.

–Yes, of course, look, here on this page is the visa –she spoke nervously at the same time that she brusquely leafed through the passport, looking for the page where her visa had been stamped. When she found it, she passed it to him, looking at him in search of a positive answer; with a firm, respectful voice and without crying, she said:

–Look, here is my visa, everything is in order, I don't understand why I'm being held here and, I'm not with my husband –she insisted and repeated again–, it's a British spouse's visa, just as you demanded of me before sending me back to Chile. My husband has been waiting for me here at the airport for more than two hours.

The policeman took his time to revise and check that everything was fine, although he obviously knew that everything was in order and that Esmeralda had the right to enter the United Kingdom. He raised his head looking at her complacently and outlining a slight smile, he asked:

–Do you want to be reunited with your husband?

–Yes, of course! –she anxiously replied.

Standing up from his seat, he took a few steps towards an adjoining door, opened it with one hand and showed her the way with the other and, turning to Esmeralda, he said, smiling:

–Come on in.

–Wow, wow!

She couldn't believe it; her beloved Terry was there in the middle of the immense room, with his arms wide open. They ran to each other, frantically hugging, crying, while saying:

–Finally... finally... we can be together! I love you; I love you!

–I love you too!

A big round of applause and emotional screams were heard, that made them react:

–Long live the bride and groom, long live the happy couple! –everyone threw rice over their heads, spreading it all over their bodies and on the floor.

–But, how? You knew what was going on as did everyone else? –she asked surprised, looking around at the police, her friend Camila, Terry's father and brother, as well as Andrew and David, Terry's friends that had been the witnesses at their wedding in Chile.

–Wow! I can't believe it, what a tremendous surprise you all had planned for me; you all almost killed me from the nerves and worry! –she looked at Terry questioningly, and scolding him and at the same time smiling:

–And you also knew and kept it a secret?

–I'm so sorry, my love, I'm truly sorry; forgive me, please, we only wanted to give you a surprise.

–And whose idea, was it? Because I honestly don't think it was yours, my love.

Right away she looked around for her friend Camila and, pointing at her with her index finger, exclaimed raising her voice:

–It was you!!!

–Me? Why do you think it was me? –she replied with a surprised face.

They all laughed and started to open a bottle of champagne, while the chief police officer addressed them and, especially Esmeralda:

–It is a great joy and a pleasure to have met Esmeralda and know that her love story is real. I apologize and regret everything that you had to go through; however, it was our job and we had to respect the protocols. It happens daily that we detect people trying to enter the UK illegally, one of the most used strategies being to marry a Briton –shrugging his shoulders and with his palms up, he added in a lamenting tone–, I'm sorry, Esmeralda.

Esmeralda approached him and gave him a hug thanking him for his efforts. The policeman said goodbye to everyone, exclaiming:

–I have to get back to work now, but not without first joining in on the toast.

He accepted the champagne glass that George, Terry's father, offered him and, lifting it, he toasted with everyone:

¡¡¡Cheers to the bride and groom!!!

¡¡¡Cheers to the bride and groom!!!

¡¡¡Cheers to the bride and groom!!!

Printed in Great Britain
by Amazon

80724910R00220